Killing Goliath

Killing Goliath

Waging War Against the New World Order

Written by Jeffrey Alexander Hamilton

iUniverse, Inc.

New York Lincoln Shanghai

Killing Goliath
Waging War Against the New World Order

iUniverse books may be ordered through booksellers or by contacting:

iUniverse
2021 Pine Lake Road, Suite 100
Lincoln, NE 68512
www.iuniverse.com
1-800-Authors (1-800-288-4677)

All poems in this book were written by Jeffrey Alexander Hamilton

ISBN-13: 978-0-595-37050-4 (pbk)
ISBN-13: 978-0-595-81451-0 (ebk)
ISBN-10: 0-595-37050-0 (pbk)
ISBN-10: 0-595-81451-4 (ebk)

Printed in the United States of America

This book is first dedicated to my Lord and Savior Jesus Christ who stands by my side in spite of my downfalls. My Parents Lionel and Mazie Hamilton, sisters Cynthia and Pamela, nephew Anthony and my brother in-law Dale. I cannot forget my extended family in Texas, California, Oklahoma and everywhere else you all might end up. My Community Church of God family, My coworkers and friends in the Ann Arbor Public Schools. I can't forget my teammates from the Southern Michigan Timber Wolves, my Ransomed Heart Ministries family, my buddies in Sanchin-Ryu, fellow bodybuilders in the gym and all people working with me in some area and facet of my life (there are way too many people to name, but you're all valuable to me).

Contents

Introduction

Killing Goliath won't happen overnight. This modern day Goliath called the New World Order is exponentially larger than the human giant who was defeated by David back in the days of the Old Testament. This giant is way more ferocious, for this battle is not a physical one, but a spiritual one that seeps its way into every facet of our lives. This collection of poetry was inspired and written out of my desire to stand up against the New World Order and everything such an order promotes. The current state of America is one where We the People regardless of our age, race, sex, status or income level must band together and stand up against the wrongdoing in our government. I firmly believe that there are good people in our government, who just need to be presented with the necessary information to stand against those who seek to control and manipulate America behind the scenes. I pray that God's blessings are upon those who read this work and stand up for what is right in this world!

Jeffrey Alexander Hamilton

I've Got to Stand Up!

I can't sit silently watching my country dying
Living like a namby-pamby sucking my thumb and crying
Embracing the sissyfied notion of submission
Lending my tail end to be kicked with my own permission
Waving a flag while giving up my liberty
Pledging allegiance to criminals thus forsaking my dignity
Calling myself a Christian while running from the battle
Engaging in phony worship and useless, mindless prattle
My children shouldn't need barbwired fences at schools
Especially when they're dumbed down to become gibbering fools
It's my hope they'll maximize their intelligence
But not through learning worthless facts that are irrelevant
How can I rest easily knowing my family's imprisoned
Being told to trust Big Brother while their dreams become wizened
I may be called demented for taking a stand against tyranny
Being called one who searches for nothing but theories of conspiracy
Overall it matters little what other's may think of me
The naysayers should be thankful I'm helping them to live free
My mind is clear and empowered, I'm destined to ruffle some feathers
I've got to stand up and help awaken those too complacent in fair
    weather

No Big Bankers

These Bankers are trippin
Further into debt Americans are slippin
Clear cabinet, no food in the kitchen
Can't afford to buy no bread or chicken
Meanwhile these thugs are stuffing their faces
Wiping their dung on all of the races
Raising our taxes, our backs are broken
Leaving the family man hurt yet hoping
He can put His family under some shelter
Because he feels his world is helter-skelter
These big boys are riding high thinking they're Jesus
Feeding us from the trough thinking they'll please us
It's time for America to throw out debt creation
Burdensome plastic and illegal taxation
There's a better way for us to achieve abundant prosperity
It's through trusting God alone, not the promoters of ruthless
    barbarity

9/11

On that dreaded day the Towers fell
Men women and children witnessed manifestations of Hell
The fire blazed, the bombs exploded
Structures of American wonder were now eroded
Panic hit the streets, chaos reigned supreme
I was hoping and praying this was just a bad dream
My anger was a white hot torch blazing with ferocity
At the enemy who committed such an act of bellicosity
Not too long after my torch cooled I came to the realization
That America's true nemesis resides within our great nation
To the public and hurting families the government lied
And now our precious American freedoms are being shanghaied
Going through all this madness in the name of freedom from terror
Whoever allowed this administration in office committed a foul error
Now we're searched at airports like we're thugs and criminals
Treated as mindless slaves and being regarded as imbeciles
Big brother is not only watching, but he's intruding, harassing and
    killing
This horror story is nonfiction, which makes it so frightening and
    chilling
I stretched forth my hands and shouted out to the God of Heaven
That America will wake up to the truth about Nine-Eleven

One World Controllers

I'm tired of endless lies robbing America
Casting us all into nothing but Hysteria
Anthrax, the World Trade what's next malaria?
They'll soon find reason to send troops to Bulgaria
Elitist pricks taking innocent lives
Murdering husbands, hiting on wives
Knowing of the man with no shoes on his feet
These clowns never had to worry bout nothing to eat
Like lost little lambs we show up to vote
Hoping this man that man will row our boat
Their royal blood spits in the face of God
Beating those who oppose them to nothing but sod
Using the name of Jesus as a cover
But behind shut doors they care for no other
They rape, plunder, murder and steal
Heartless dungeaters will take a widows last meal
Inbred greedy scavengers never had responsibility
Scandalize Americans without any lawful accountability
Somehow I smell their deception getting funkier
While the Federal Reserve swine is getting chunkier

Where is Osama?

Where is the thug who took down the towers?
Is he the same one raining down chemical warfare like April showers?
I'm no war guru but based on my thought out analysis
It should be simple to find a tall bearded man on dialysis
Like a prarie dog underground in and out his head keeps on popping
When the globalists have a wicked plan they're concocting
Such as getting our children prepared for military selection
Or making sure another pirate gets a boost for an election
In 1963 they can easily knock off John F. Kennedy
Yet today in hi-tech America, they can't find Osama? Now that's a
  mystery
For the umpteenth time we've been deceived and conned
They have no heartfelt to desire to capture that man
Especially when he's an asset they consistently rely on
To help carry out their Imperialistic, sadisitic, and fuedalistic plan
So if you ever wonder where's the nations most notorious lawbreaker
He's probably being protected by some crooked elitist bankers!

Wake Up Please!

What's wrong with this picture
It keeps going out of focus
Looks like a propagandist fixture
America's been hit by locusts
So in utter desperation
We take what we're given
A choice between two skeletons
Once again by the Serpent we've been bitten
The venom has damaged our brain
To where we can't properly think
Our Constitution is going down the drain
We're clogged up and starting to stink
A funk so retchedly foul
The whole world is choking on our fumes
The night wolves have howled
And the helpless deer are doomed
Slowly bleeding and dying from attack
We've being infected by brainwash disease
Spent too much time dreaming and lying on our backs
That's why my cry to America is: wake up please!

A Mission for the Brave

I have a disdain for foul and gross iniquity
Especially for young girls being treated so despicably
Lured away from the comfort of their very home
Sold into prostitution before they're grown
Tossed around and treated like chattel
Entangled in a horrid and nightmarish battle
Broken, abused, beaten and molested
In a ring of evil that's disease infested
Praying for a deliverer to brake their chains
And give them freedom from sorrow, torment and pain
I can't let my life slowly fade away
And let these precious children rot and decay
May curses demolish my world if I don't stand and fight
Against this putrid evil that's vile in God's sight
I'll ransom my prosperity for even one to be saved
This mission won't be for the weak but for the valiantly brave

Precious Baby Will You Remember Me?

Precious baby looking up at me
I wish you could clearly express what you see
Deep down I wonder what you'll remember-
Of me, if I should be killed on this day in November
Will you recall when I held you high?
Showing you off to the birds in the sky
Proclaiming God's goodness in giving me such a blessing
With a smile so precious my heart was deliquescing
I leave you this message I pray you'll understand
That daddy paid the price of being a front line man
Who couldn't be there to see you flourish and grow
Teaching you how to read the Bible or pick up a ball and throw
Let me make this clear before my tears get ahead of me
It's my hearts desire to leave behind a legacy
One of hope, freedom, justice and abundant prosperity
Not one of despair, hunger, decadence and scarcity
One day you'll realize the price of liberty is life itself
And know that you can be in bondage with abundant wealth
When the leaves are falling on the anniversary of that November
I wonder, what about me will you truly remember?

United States of Criminals

Robbed and left with little though we work so hard
Drained of our lively-hood being fit only for the graveyard
Bills piling up, people calling and harassing for collections
Lawyers being bought off leaving us with little protection
Outsourcing jobs claiming it helps the economy
While the super rich fatten their pockets creating bigger monopolies
Hoarding up treasures not fit for the Kingdom of Heaven
While poisoning our troops with chemical warfare weapons
Imperialism is their longing and lustful desire
Engulfing sovereign and innocent states and setting them on blazing
    fire
Never mind the slaughtered elderly, women and children of those
    nations
For by the Elite's standards the blameless are worthy of incrimination
These global thugs say we must engage in these wars
Parading around the globe like 16th-Century conquistadors
More youth will die in battles for which they're unprepared
Under the guise of American liberty to commit atrocities beyond
    repair
These malefactors will decapitate whoever opposes their agenda
We've become the United States of Criminals, now ain't that quite a
    dilemma?

Victory's Story

My head is throbbing from the lies I keep hearing
From a rogue administration and all these people cheering
Pumping their fists waving American flags made in Hong Kong
Being enticed and led into evil by the siren's song
Will they ever see the radiant light of factuality?
Or is ignorance too much of a safe haven from reality
When I show them the evidence of our nation being plundered
They stare at me clueless like I'm some delusional drunkard
When the cold gaze has ended it seems as nothing's changed
And I wonder if I wasted valuable time on such an interchange
Though at times I get discouraged, the Lord reminds me
To keep on with my message even when I'm inclined to be-
Somewhat let down with the results I'm receiving-
I'll refocus on God and in my heart continue believing-
That there is a remnant who will stand for His glory
Warring boldly against tyranny playing a part in Victory's story

Guilty for Murder and Treason!

Now wouldn't Hitler be pleased if he were living today?
Seeing the madness happening in the USA
Militarizing the streets that everybody is walking
Somehow I feel as if Big Brother keeps stalking-
My every move, even breaths that I breathe
Wouldn't be a surprise if he counted my very heartbeat
Through some hi-tech odorless microscopic device
Used by mad scientists made for rats and mice
Forcible testing for mental illness to drug our children
We're chasing Middle Easterners, but who's the real villain?
The Patriot Act urinates on our Constitution
Opening up an unimaginable wave of persecution
On the people who are supposed to be liberated
Ending up robbed, beaten down and mutilated
What I write in this rhyme may come as a surprise
But I feel the threat of Nazi Germany on the rise
Nine-Eleven should serve as an early wake up call
That we cannot trust these Neocons at all
Using the name of Jesus to promote the work of Satan
The disheartening reality, is that it's so repugnant and blatant
Our eyes can no longer be blinded to the game-
That these felons continue to play to our shame
Give me just a minute and I'll provide more than one reason
Why this administration is guilty for murder and treason!

IRS: Illegal Repugnant Slavery

They're running wild like animals out of control
Plundering the American peoples wealth they stole
Brutal tacticians masters of their wicked art
Don't care about all the families they tore apart
Mid April the panic button sounds the alarm
The mob is out and ready to harass and harm-
Old people, stuggling mothers's, it really doesn't matter
If one is on life support they still will be shattered-
By bullies who don't realize their day is imminent
To where they'll have to pay for terrorizing the innocent
When will we cry that enough is enough?
We won't take anymore of being treated so rough
No more being threatened by this criminal creation
So called "federal" but just an organization-
Designed to keep Americans bound in their fear
To rob them of their wealth in a controlled atmosphere
Fraudulent, scandalous, thieves of prosperity
You've been warned by the Lord of your wrong with severity
We the people must take up arms with bravery-
And pray that God empowers us to fight this illegal repugnant slavery!

Radical Feminism: America's Biggest Joke

Please oh please think of what you're saying!
Beefed up on chicken hormones pretty soon eggs you'll be laying
Shouting out your vocal chords for so called liberation
Forcing your man into undesirable hibernation
This media madness has wrecked your cognition
Rendering you with little more than a sour disposition
Feeding you the lies of so-called equality
Knowing all the propaganda is nothing but frivolity
"Do without a man" is the message they sell
Even when you're bench pressing twice your weight with the barbell-
In the gym you're now stronger than him, ready to fight
But let me bring you back to earth with a little insight
You were created in the image of God the Father
So any argument about equality ain't even worth the bother
If some clown can't appreciate your God given beauty
He's not worth trying to convince, thus it's not your duty
Take a moment and recognize the reality of your essence
Founded in Eden's Garden, it's time for your rejuvenescence
These tongue flappin' anti-family minions disdain your very nature
The same tall tales are being told to your depressed and lonely
    neighbor
Deprive not the world of the loveliness that you alone possess
A beauty so enticing and powerful to which even the mightiest man
    must acquiesce
It's my burning desire that through these few words I will evoke
A passion for true womanhood not radical feminism, that is,
    America's biggest joke!

Keep Your Hands Off of My Precious Children!

Keep your hands off my precious little children
I won't let you enslave them to the new world you're buildin'
Mind control dynamics are making them crazy
Drugged out on psychotropics making them passive and lazy
Labeling them with all sorts of funny initials
So you can manufacture more poison to make their brains sizzle
Our nutrition is destroyed by foul agents and chemicals
Destroying rational cognition, producing a nation of criminals
Vaccinations for kids are now forcibly required
While at the same time more funny farms have been acquired-
To house those who happen to be severely autistic
Viewing them as subhuman, worthless and sadistic
If a little boy thinks differently, he's put on some potion
Then the dose is doubled if he displays his emotions
It's not my place to say medication is never needed
Yet it appears as if wise limits have been exceeded
Every little child doesn't need to be medicinally burdened
So the drug companies bottom line can be guerdoned
Touch my child and you can bet we will rumble
Hitting and kicking hard in a battle that's rough-and-tumble
You'll taste the flavor of my knuckles in your mouth
And you can best believe that you'll be heading south
When you look up at me you'll realize I wasn't kiddin'
When I told you the first time to keep your hands off my precious
children

God's Blessed Sanctuary

The preacher spoke on a "secret place"
A peaceful habitation where a man can seek the Lord's face
David had fought hard on the battlefield
For the sake of God's glory, he refused to yield
Though victorious, he was battered, bruised and tired
Every ounce of zest, passion and zeal had expired
He knew the presence of God was a place where he could dwell
To find restoration, rejuvenation and serenity from the forces of Hell
In my fight against the New World Order
Serving my land and family as a godly warder
It gets lonely, frustrating, hard and heavy at times
Fighting against those indulging in lustful crimes
I slump in the bed after a long day of being battered and worn
Feeling as if I've been attacked by a beast and torn
When I've had enough of fighting the adversary
I turn in and thus find refuge in the presence of God's blessed
    Sanctuary

My Justifiable Objection

I refuse to take part in President Bush's war
Even if they do extend the draft age to 34
There's no way I'm destroying my wonderful life
Spoiling a chance I have at a future wife-
And a quiver full of children to carry around
Pointing them to God the Father so their life will abound-
With blessings so they can be a contributor-
Of good to the world, they'll be Gospel distributors
If we're attacked on America soil
I'll be compelled to fight knowing it's not for oil
But for life, liberty and love for family
Not for the New World Order's flimflammery
We're being drained of our blessed posterity
Now we're known across the world for our vile barbarity
When my number comes up in this unrighteous service selection
I'll politely refuse stating my justifiable objection

Jeffrey Alexander Hamilton

Throw Off the Yoke!

If I may express my politically incorrect opinion
I'm not cool with having my world controlled by Satan's minions
Implanting computer chips into my brain to read my emotions
Bound to cause damage through cerebral implosions
Spying through the walls of my house watching my every activity
Trying to force me into their global captivity
Everyplace I go more cameras are being placed-
Up above my head to watch my every move and trace
Transmitting my personal information to Big Brother
From where I went to school to the maiden name of my mother
What's next a flying camera posing as a bug?
Or are they working on a mind controlling airborne drug?
The Elite desire to cast an invisible net on the population
To keep us trapped in their worldwide slave plantation
That way they'll prevent all legitimate rebellions
Labeling Patriots as Communists and Christians as Hellions
They'll open up a grand execution chamber
To throw in any slave they feel is a danger-
And threat to the hellish order they wish to institute
It's far past time for Americans to depollute-
These devil worshiping thugs, brutes and killers
Before they turn us over to be ground like grain by the millers
True Americans, keep your sword by your side
Because far too many of our people have needlessly died-
In so called "wars" to establish peace and liberation
Which have done nothing more than gutted our very nation
The time for revolution is this moment before we're in too deep
Our generation knows abundant freedom, but doesn't realize liberty
    isn't cheap

We're being flooded by too many taxes, abuses and open borders
Let's pull together and throw off the yoke of the New World Order

National Salvation

Wake up fellow Christians let's rise from our slumber
It's past time to pull back the covers we've been hiding under
Left and right people are being led to the slaughter
But we could care less, it's not our sons or daughters
Showered in materialism has rendered us weak
Our testimony to the world around us has started to reek-
Of a smell horrid enough to make a skunk shrink away and hide
Our country's dying and we're sitting on our backsides
We fell into the trap of being overly trusting and tender
That we'll cheer on the nations biggest criminal offenders
Somehow we've cast away true knowledge and wise discernment
Which is why so many will be headed to camps of internment-
Right here in this great country that we're living in
Too afraid to fight so we make a habit of giving in-
To whatever the Government affirms as policy
While behind the scenes our so called leaders engage in diablerie
Born once we came into a world at war
Born a second time we need to echo the Lion's roar-
And take to the battlefield representing our Father
No more being effeminate it's time stir up a pother
Setting the captives free and spreading liberation
For where the Lord's spirit is, there is soul and national salvation

A Land of Freedom and Dignity

Enough is finally a thousand miles far past enough

We're fifteen past the midnight hour it's time get tough

Let's make these legislatures do as they promise

The people are the reason they get to warm their backsides in chairs of
congress

Chump change is minimum wage, just barely enough to buy bread

Try filling your tank with those wages, you'll end up riding a bike to
work instead

Meanwhile insurance has neglected millions of poor children

But somehow these same kids end up in new prison cells we're buildin'

More pills are passed out at school, yet our nutrition is depleted

We wonder why children can't concentrate walking around feeling
defeated

If a man can't provide for his family he takes a blow to his heart and
passion

And memories of better moments he dwells upon and starts his ole'
rehashin'

Yet when he's able to bring home the bread, bacon and butter

He'll gladly sit down with his wife and kids enjoying their company
along with supper

The bottom line of this message that from my heart I'm conveying

America is going straight to Hell, we need to be involved more deeply
than just praying

It's not that prayer to God doesn't have the power to shake mountains
loose

But prayer in our world has become nothing more than a convenient
excuse-

To avoid the pressing issues that are troubling our land of liberty

It's time for being bold, let's make America a land of freedom and
dignity

Second Revolution of the USA

Welcome to the second American Revolution

These criminal minded tyrants are nothing more than pollution

Spreading diseased mechanisms across the states

Leaving us with limbs ready to amputate

Soldiers poisoned, kids overdosing on pills

Bodies in war are being tossed into putrid landfills

Why do we persist in continuing to blindly follow?

Men whose minds are bent toward evil, with hearts so hollow

All under the guise of being free from some reprobate

So the government can oppress us with new laws that they mandate

Being patted down before taking a flight

Or getting tracked down by some intrusive satellite

We've all become suspects of crime on this global plantation

And we're supposed to show Big Brother our appreciation-

For locking us up in shackles over minuscule crimes

Then going on TV with their nursery rhymes-

About how drugs are bad and how they'll kill you

But if you stand up to whose behind those same drugs, they'll grill you

I'll make this sermon short simple, the crooked Elite had better make
way

Freedom fighters are on the rise ready to launch the second Revolution
of the USA

We Desire to Be Understood

Ladies of the world will you ever understand?
Or take the time to read the heart of a real man?
Realize first that he cares for more than mere sex
When I say this to some I sense some disconnect
Often our emotions are hidden or damaged by erosion
Packed tightly within the heart ready cause an implosion
The Radical Feminist have done our culture tremendous damage
Wounding firm godly family units, yet unwilling to provide bandage-
Leaving open sores only fit for infestation, germs and disease
Is it any wonder men have become the notorious absentees?
To our wives, children, extended family and friends
Stuck from nine to five with an ungrateful supervisor in a job that's
    dead-end
Seeing dreams die and afraid to open up and express-
How the pain cuts so deep and causes so much distress-
Bleeding slowing our vitality's tremendously expired
Home from work we hit the bed from being beat up and tired
When we're slumbering soundly it doesn't mean we don't love you
Because in reality we think more than the entire Universe of you
Let me let you in on a secret about manhood-
Though we're different from you we too desire to be understood

Stand Guard!

What's happening in our world with all these nasty child slaying's

Predators lurking around dark corners, on little boys and girls their preying

Disappearing by the thousands nowhere to be found-

But left battered, bruised and sometimes beheaded and buried underground

Stolen from their beds at night one can only imagine where they're taken

Sad to say their lives are snuffed out; it's in Heaven where they'll be reawakened

Though God's presence is a place of comfort for precious lives cut short

The pain of losing one so young is the heaviest heartache to abort

I've reached my threshold of tolerance with these senseless acts of murder

Even mad at myself for hearing such news, barely flinching and stuffing my face with a burger

Who am I not to shed a tear, feel pain or drop to my knees and pray?

For a family with shattered emotions, even if they do live far away

I'm through with the worn out, sorry and lame excuses for not being involved

Such as "the problem's to big for one person, so why bother, it'll never get solved"

God's children are a gift to us, a beloved and priceless treasure

With a value that reaches to Heaven, with such a worth that's beyond measure

The Devil's on a rampage possessing minds to wipe out those who need protection

We must submit to God and make our kids the objects of our deepest affections

For if we don't the judgment we face will be nothing less than no-holds-barred

Take my words seriously, consecrate your children to the Lord, be vigilant and stand guard!

Deathblow!

Check this out, I saw a lady looking kind of crazy
With her were six or seven little precious babies
She sold one to a man for a quick little hit
Poor three year old girl paid the price for it
Plugged in too early ravished and traumatized by the fella
Cold hearted, and uncompassionate, better yet plain yella
Violating a precious little flower not even opened yet
Just a while ago she was laying in a bassinet
What will she think of men now and when she gets older?
She's the victim of society that's grown distant and colder
Now she can't stand, walk a straight line
Pain in the back, damage to the spine
Not able to sleep going through body spasms
No little girl should ever be forced into an orgasm
I ask God for His mercy for being planted on my behind
While little children are violated by my own kind
Who is my own kind? That would be society's men
For if I sit silently, I'm just as guilty for such sin
Maybe not so much by the act of commission
But shame upon my world, for the sin of omission
I can't imagine for one millisecond if she were my daughter
Quite honestly, I'd be tempted to drag that malefactor to the slaughter
It would take Jesus to strengthen me and remind me that He will
    repay
I hope I never endure such devastation, anyhow let me not get carried
    away

For this to happen in our backyard, demonstrates we've reached an all
time low
Let's ban our hearts and minds together and deal child molestation a
piercing deathblow

Jeffrey Alexander Hamilton

Rise Up America!

We've riled up many nations provoking them to anger
Somehow I feel in my heart we're in deep danger
Not so much from the enemies abroad
But from those within claiming they're serving God
The nation was strong when families were together
Now we're being divided by a conspiracy so clever-
That one day the whole world will be a global unit
Forcing us into unisex mind sets, turning us into eunuchs
This is the moment to fight for our community
Band against the tyrants who scoff at godly unity
Be ready to lay it on the line for our flesh and blood
Rather than living our whole lives stuck in the mud
Every moment we procrastinate precious time's ticking away
Drawing closer to our country falling to decay
Let's rise up now while the Illuminati are out manned
Before they turn our great country into a wasteland

Run These Varmints Out of Town!

Prepare your horses for battle, stand firm against the coming crisis
Step out of your comfort zone, quit hiding behind the curtain of
    niceness
We are standing on the brink of a horrendous depression
Stemming from this vile ongoing tyrannical global oppression
The Federal Reserve brought ruin to our nation
Playing their part in worldwide dictatorship and colonization
Internal Revenue Service is nothing but a fraud and a joke
Crushing families with cumbersome burdens and strangulating yokes
Gas is overpriced, prescription prices keep soaring
We've been victimized by the bull and he keeps on goring-
Leaving us bloody, too broken and bruised for battle
Too far into consumer debt we're being made into chattel
Trillions from the people the Fed keeps on bilking
When the banks shut their doors there'll be folks jumping off
    buildings
Let us all ban together before America goes down
It's past time we run these Varmints out of town!

Jeffrey Alexander Hamilton

Pull Together

What's happening with these gas prices today going crazy?
Concerning the rationale for such madness I'm a bit hazy
Prescription prices being quadrupled are bad enough to face
That along with crude oil and my whole income's erased
What do these thugs need with more of my money?
Trying to bring cloud cover to my world that's glowing and sunny
For when the light shines brightly their deception is exposed
Igniting the fury of the American people that they oppose
We're broke at the gas tank, bankrupt from the physician
Made sick from our groceries leading us into malnutrition
Property taxes, heavy interest on our houses
Pressing us into parting way with our spouses
Divorce is a killer, leaving a debt insurmountable
Couples need to bond closely and hold these thugs accountable
We need to flood the members of congress
With letters, emails, phones calls and do it with firm promptness
This mad and crazy situation is past out of control
Elite conspirators doing nothing more than fattening their bankroll
We're heading for a time of severe inclement weather
It'll be a bloody fight, that's why we must pull together

A Glorious Dream

Last night in my sleep I dreamt that there was liberty
All across America people were free from Tyranny
Gas prices were reasonable, prescription costs decreased
There was life in the Constitution that once was deceased
No police state in fact the cops were law abiding-
Husbands and fathers working hard steady providing-
Food for the table, clothes upon the back
Ready to die for the family if they were under attack
A wife and mother working was optional, not an obligation
Mom was now available to provide godly education-
To the children who weren't tagged and treated as a number
Having a blessed school year, ready to play in Summer-
Yes they could play outside till the night took over
Playing classic games like Freeze Tag, Mr. Fox and Red Rover
Not being plopped in front of the tube for stimulation
TV was limited for special moments during vacation
Then again families were too busy out walking and hiking
Enjoying family reunions, church barbeques playing ball and biking
If they gathered to watch TV a show, it was based in ethical intent
Not the kind of garbage rendering children morally impotent
Our kids weren't drugged and given alphabet labels
The media was legitimate not a breeding ground of fables
School was a place were free ideas and thoughts we're the norm
Not a government slave system in need of reform
Republicans, Democrats, Constitutionalists, and Libertarians
All banned together becoming disestablishmentarians-
That is if there was an inkling of globalism on the rise
I looked up above me, there were no aerosol tainted skies
Everybody could praise and worship God without threat
All were well off, no one even heard of consumer debt

Then abruptly I was awaken by the harsh reality
That what I experienced last night was routed in ideality
Rather than be disheartened, disappointed and depressed
I prayed to God, asking for forgiveness where I've transgressed
For if my most glorious dream will ever come to fruition
I must start with myself and let God be the captain of my life's mission

Until This World Is Through

Young man please hear me, I'm trying to set you straight
It's my aim to keep you from meeting a harsh and deadly fate
Although you think I'm your enemy for getting in your face
One day you realize what a friend I was to you and the end of life's race
There's a world waiting for you that desires to lock you away
Which is why I remember you every moment when I take the time to
    pray
My prayer is that you'll have knowledge to weather life's hurricanes
Be strong through the mountains and valleys and yes, the growing
    pains
Now is the time that is set before you to lay a solid foundation
That will keep you strong in your daily walk onto your destination
Give your life over to the Lord, so your life will be made right
Then you'll learn of a great battle that's worth your very best fight
Don't let this moment pass without making such a critical decision
Making the Lord captain of your ship and director of you provision
If ever there was a moment I went overboard in how I dealt with you
Please forgive me and keep in mind that I'm on your side until this
    world is through

The Obligations of Conquest

Egomaniacal, psychopathic truth evaders
Imperialistic, colonizing cruel slave traders
We can't allow our future in this country to be handled-
By a few insane elite who leave us dismantled
Sound the alarm, take up your swords, call the brigade
Let's take back America while these clowns are outweighed-
Out manned, outwitted and plain out of options
Realizing they're not all powerful, but here's a caution-
This war won't be won merely by man made weaponry
Victory will only be certain with this recipe:
Submit to the Lord God, add in righteous prayer
Study what's in His word, but here's another layer
Learn of world history, gather valid information
Share with family, friends, co-workers and radio stations-
Television, internet and ecclesiastical institutions
It's time the people fight in a godly revolution
Let the fainthearted remain at home sitting on their couches
Complaining about what isn't right as do slouching grouches
The real men valiant of heart are ready for the contest
And won't surrender until they fulfill the obligations of conquest

Front Line Man

Lord, with all of this madness surrounding me, how can I remain
  silent?

I'm not thinking so much about being vengeful, hateful or violent

But it seems to me that when it comes to American Christians

Too many of us embrace the idea that everyday our path should
  glisten-

And never be burdened with the thought of battle or even slight
  opposition

It's about this time in history that evangelical minds be reconditioned-

To realize that walking in freedom carries a backbreaking price

Which is why I'll start with myself and ask you Lord to make me right

I need not utter words of complaint about the world while planted on
  my rear

When I've been blessed to walk, breathe, see, have my right mind and
  hear

Should I not be one who stands boldly against those hurting the
  fatherless?

Or will I cuss at the TV screen, hold my head down and walk around
  in somberness

If troops are being dismembered, crippled, overtaxed and killed by
  depleted uranium

And I care for nothing more than who won the game, will someone
  please examine my cranium?

Women and children being trafficked throughout every continent, to
  live as slaves

When they're all washed up, they're dismembered or tossed into
  disease infested mass graves

What will the extent of my judgment be if I run and hide from the
  war?

One thing I know is that a divine spanking leaves much more than
  bruises and sores

So dear Jesus I repent and ask you to forgive me for not staunchly taking a stand-

For good and against evil, since your mercy is new everyday, please make me a front line man

Homeland Insecurity

If this so called nationwide bodyguard is legitimate
Then why must I be one to show a paper certificate?
To a man dressed in black with no badge number
This new system exceeds the definition of a foul blunder
Am I really safe from enemies from abroad
When open borders allow for a psychopathic jihad
Who are we defending against if Americans are suspects
Being pushed around instead of defended by leathernecks
Our military is desperately being overextended
Being used in ways never previously intended
Suddenly this rogue renegade department's created
And now American citizens rights have been abnegated
High school students arrested, the elderly get beaten
People blacklisted as terror suspects for holding a secret meetin'
Now when the Elite hold a session it gets hidden in obscurity
Yet We the People are imprisoned by Homeland Insecurity

PNAC: Pathetic New American Crack Heads

It seems apparent that you were high when you drafted this document

Perhaps your brain is warped by habitual crimes and fraudulence

When I last checked, smoking and dealing with crack were illegal

But oh yeah now I remember you all are above the law royal and regal

By conquering sovereign nations who'll be paying the penalty?

Kids drafted straight out of high school to be slain and damaged mentally

Left with little to nothing not even health insurance

After putting on the camouflage and being stretched beyond their own endurance

If you drafters of this document are so concerned with conquest

You throw on a uniform, load up your cartridge and hope you don't get blasted in the chest

What's your apprehension? Doesn't a real man fight for liberty?

Or are you too caught up living with luxury under a facade of dignity?

If somebody hurts my family, community or country, they've engaged in war with me

Yet I'll be at peace with an innocent citizen living in a place with established sovereignty

Didn't you all know that drugs do major damage to your health?

Breaking up families and robbing a man of his precious hard earned wealth?

You've caused much destruction to those in the Middle East

Leaving elderly, women and little children decapitated and deceased

You all must be smoking something terrible to carry out what you're doing

You New American Crack-Heads need to repent, for you've caused our nation much ruin!

Gumption In My Veins

I got up one morning looked in the mirror realizing I haven't done a
thing

About dying soldiers, false imprisonments and children been thrown
into sex slave rings

I had the raw audacity to get caught up in my pride about giving away
a few dollars-

To aid those who are starving and being penetrated while letting out
a terrifying squaller

I claim to care for and love the children, but what true sacrifice have I
made-

To rescue even one from a horror filled existence, by being distant and
afraid?

Meanwhile my neighbor was dragged off to prison for a crime of
which he's innocent-

In broad daylight in front of his kids, instead of shrugging my
shoulders I should be indignant

Ready to defend my neighbor that's wronged, abused, beaten and
humiliated

If Jesus protects and stands for me why can't I stand for others who
falsely incriminated

Wasn't I blessed with my strength for protecting the weak and
harmless?

Not to gloat over my power and then go live my life in a self-centered
harness

My accountability to God for sitting silent is far beyond humiliating

I need to confess my sins and repent this day, no more procrastinating

When I meditate on all those who suffer by virtue of my refusal to ease
their pains

In repentance, I ask God to forgive me and put some gumption in my
veins!

Poisoned!

I can't quite understand the modern American diet
This garbage is so foul every conscious citizen should start a riot
Complain to the FDA about being contaminated
I believe this is a planned population reduction so carefully
    contemplated
Teenage girls with breast big enough to asphyxiate an elephant
Through gorging on and chugging down all kinds of weird elements
Like hydrogenated products and other words hard to enunciate
It's no wonder they're so ready to get busy and start to procreate
We wrestle with cancer, diabetes and heart disease
Steroid induced cows giving us chemical beef, milk and cheese
Pesticides on my apple, I think I'd prefer chewing on the bug
What's worse an adulterated peach or a nice juicy North American
    slug?
Bleached flour? Why not just give us Clorox to drink straight?
Or is dying slowly from the inside out our rendezvous with fate?
With so much illness we need a nutritional revolution
To rid our diets of this edible poisonous biological pollution!

War of Information

We're on a collision course with disaster and a major cataclysm
Many thanks unto those maniacal architects of globalism
Our world is much better without these men in power
Criminal minds turn the sweet and pure taste of America sour
Debt is a disaster, cars, houses and tuition are too expensive
Americans must band together and form a counteroffensive-
Against this tyrannical and thieving new world system
Upholding the Constitution and being led by God's wisdom
My fear is that we don't know the very price of emancipation
Being blessed with tons of luxury and two-week vacations
Why should the previous generations shed blood and we sit silent?
Are we too afraid of bloodshed, getting rough and a little violent?
At the very least let's do something for our descendants
When it concerns their future, on us they are dependent
Let us never forget the sacrifice made for our autonomy
To some I know this message is no more than cacophony
But for those ready for an engagement long, hard, and deadly
Who will lean upon God to uphold and keep them steady
Join with me in liberating our fantastic nation
By getting involved in the War of Information

Ready to Fight!

I'm the watchman, the guard dog of the flock
I patrol the border pacing back and forth on the dock
Come near the fatherless, you're bound to be bitten
Touch the crippled man then you will be smitten
I'm called to protect and defend those hurt and bruised
Ones who can't see straight, the bedridden and misused
My purpose is not taking vengeance on my enemy
But defending the helpless with godly intensity
Manhood embraces the balance of being tough and tender
We men have lost sight of the splendor of our gender
Being the nice guy has replaced being the leader
Now the woman has become the rock and the superceder
I have been called by my heavenly Father
To boldly declare His truth, not tone down and become softer
I like the Jesus in the Bible who took the whip-
Unto the cheating money changers masquerading good churchman-
ship
Not so much the Jesus portrayed in some pictures
With no manliness, but a somewhat feminine fixture
I often wish we'd bring back the days of chivalrous knights
When men could love thoroughly, but also be ready to fight!

God, Please Forgive Our Insanity

God bless you Terri, I'm praying for your victory
I can't imagine your pain and you being treated so despicably
You speak to many people though some don't comprehend-
Every single syllable, that doesn't give us the right to condescend-
And think less of you in the struggle that you're enduring
Each and every step you take forward is quite reassuring
You have life, that only God can give and take away
If our nation lets you die painfully, then a heavy price we'll have to pay
I'm sure the lovers of Hitler are smiling watching you suffer
These torture minded clowns would be black and blue if I were your
    brother
You're a champion for all those fighting for life
Seeing you in agony must cut deeper than the sharpest knife
Chugging gallons of water and eating good food daily
We in good health take so much for granted and it's flat out crazy-
That America seems to have little value for humanity
The Lord keep you Terri, and God please forgive our insanity

Investing In Eternity

Though I grind daily trying to make it on earth
I can't lose sight of that which has sustaining worth
Silver, gold and platinum may be precious to some
I admit all three have value, but here's where I'm coming from
Eternal life is an existence that's sustaining
Thus I must maximize my short life on earth that is remaining
Caring for people and the state of their salvation
Leading them to the one who gives true liberation
While on this journey I must repent of sin and error
Standing for righteousness while fighting tyranny and terror
I must confess at times I catch fire and go overboard-
With the things I say that may cut like a sword
I hope those I wounded with the poison of my tongue
Will bounce back from my blunder and recover their emotions I
    hamstrung
Lord help me please live a life of courage and certainty
Blessing people in this life and thus investing in eternity

Uprising

Ripped off and robbed daily at the gas pump
Punched, body slammed and drop-kicked into the murky dump
Left with a couple of dollars enough to buy some tacos
Break them up, throw on some Kraft cheese to make nacho's
Paying so much for prescriptions, I think I'd rather suffer
Than spend my paycheck on chemical's that'll put me under-
The cold and lonely grave, locked in a casket
Work hard everyday, yet can't afford to fill up a grocery basket
In church I want to give offering, but I can only give a minimal-
Of what I have left, for most has been taken by global criminals
It's time to bang on the doors and demand the attention of congress
March down the Mall in DC fighting hard till we see progress-
In a godly and positive direction for our remaining country
Paying workers decent wages and making sure none go hungry
Allowing for free thinking in our system of education
Rather than mind-controlling the young to hinder their liberation
The propaganda they've been force fed, they've sadly ingested
Now they're like walking clones and marionettes from the lies they
    digested
America's a ship that's been led into deep water and is capsizing
For those of us not yet drowned, we need a Biblical and Constitutional
    uprising

Worth Going to Battle for

We're no longer people anymore

But merely cattle more like chattel eating out the trough and off the floor

You and I don't have a name,

Yet we're black and white chess pieces used for pleasure in a global game

Our kids are no longer ours

But being made for psychiatric drugs and living life behind prison bars

From our job we can't retire

One paycheck from being without a home standing over a trash can fire

Our marriages aren't secure

Always seconds from divorce bombarded with adulterous thoughts so impure

How do we keep our children protected?

When government finds ways to keep the family from being closely connected

Can we keep enough food on the table?

Living with a manipulated currency and an economy so uncertain and unstable

Will We the People win this war?

Yes we will, because life and liberty are worth going to battle for!

My Fellow Negro's

What's up my fellow Negro's? You enjoying your new color?

Now you have a lil' taste of what it's like to be a brotha'

Didn't think you'd ever be here? Well here you are today

In a nation where all people are becoming victimized prey

Remember when you walked past me and chose not to speak

Now I'm your buddy, because you too are trying to make ends meet

How bout' when I tried to date your daughter? In my face you closed the door

Claiming that because I'm dark as night I'd treat her like a whore

Now that I'm paid well living a life that's good having shrimp and steak for dinner

You're on her case asking her why she passed up a proven winner!

What happened last night were you victimized by the wicked Patriot Act?

You scoffed at me when talking bout' police brutality, now you feel the impact

Homeland security harassed your son, merely for sharing his thoughts?

Life ain't fair when you're doing the right thing and you still receive a cheap shot-

From the government or some narrow minded, ignorant and racist clown

Being told in covert signs and languages that "we don't want you in this town!"

Welcome to my neighborhood, here were are together in a global penitentiary-

Or plantation, if you like being called a slave, oh yeah that's not politically correct in this century

So when you leave me behind, buddy up with Big Brother and he puts
  you on your back
You be painfully reminded in this Brave New World that your new
  color is black

Endure

I heard the voice of Jesus tell me that I have a cross to bear
For such was confirmed for me in His written Word and I said this
    prayer:
Dear heavenly Father I know your mission for me won't be an easy
    road
At times I'll feel as if I'm about to break from bearing such a load
But you'll be there to strengthen my every muscle, joint and bone
And lead me in the right direction here on earth until I'm called home.
Quite honestly it's no comfort to think of suffering persecution
Or even worse, the possibility of going through a vicious execution
Please protect my family, and I hope they're made right with you
And grow in grace being covered by your blood thus being made
    brand new
If I should not see my children grow, please help them understand
That bearing a cross is no walk in the park, it's life greatest demand
Holy Spirt, please teach them that true life is living for the Lord
Having the strength to forsake worldliness and take hold of heavenly
    rewards
Bearing my own cross daily is where I must grow and mature
And live without fear of harm, but trust Jesus, fight for good and
    endure

Culture of Death

Kill Terri! We might as well just say

Aren't we being inconvenienced by her suffering, so why delay?

She doesn't fit into this New World plan, she's taking up too much
space

Nobody will miss a half human, she needs to be erased

What value does she add to the world? It's not like she can walk

Her speech has no value, for she cannot even talk!

Who wants to be around a vegetable that cannot sit up straight?

Is she just a retard who won't intelligibly communicate?

Hold on one minute! This beautiful woman has the right to live

Just because she can't get around like us doesn't mean she has nothing
to give

Her smile is worth more than gold and she does have precious
significance

Diamonds don't compare to the worth of her life of magnificence

She's a fighter, an inspiration for us all of what it means to endure

We're the ones whose minds are diseased and looking for a cure

May God forgive us for torturing Terri to her very last breath

America the beautiful has become a culture of death

Beautiful Woman

Nothing grips a man's whole being like a woman in the nude
To some I'm going overboard and just being plain crude
But consider the number of families ruined by pornography
Through addiction to a lovely image captured in touched up
    photography
It's natural for men young and old to be draw in through the eyes
So when we turn our head gazing at voluptuous curves it should be no
    surprise
Warm tingling rising up on the inside, there's no parallel sensation
Making fantasies and ocean inhabited dreams such a preoccupation
The problem with our minds is that we're often consumed with lust
Uncontrolled hunger pangs for the backside, sacred door and busts
I know that through Christ a woman's beauty can be appreciated
Then our thoughts won't stand condemned when our thinking is
    liberated
The curse of sin has tarnished our view of God's precious creation
Can't be around a pretty woman for one minute without the hint of
    sexual temptation
Seeing a woman's form gives us clues to her natural essence
Such as her tenderness, nurturing touch and warm passion of her
    presence
It's hard to fight for purity in an age where women are objectified
But it's worth the very battle if the God in Heaven is to be glorified
Yes, a beautiful woman in her natural form will always be appealing to
    our gaze
Which is why such a breathtaking image remains in our mind for
    many days
It's critical that we as men treat the feminine kind with respect
Learn the art of self-control through the Holy Spirit, thus keeping our
    desires in check

And then upon that day when God gives us our long anticipated treat
We'll enjoy true love within the bounds of holy matrimony with a
    beautiful woman so sweet

War on Terror?

This War on Terror seems incredibly ambiguous

A group of clearly defined suspects seems awfully nebulous

First Osama Bin Laden, next Saddam Hussein

Bouncing back and forth between these two men that both are insane

Who's next on the list? Who must we pulverize?

Shall we hook their genitals to electric currents after they're
sodomized?

Perhaps we can rape their women or children as they scream?

After all aren't we above obeying the law since we are the mighty
sovereign supreme?

If my life and family are in constant danger, I'll be the first to take up
arms

Be suited up at dawn while everyone else is snoring, I'll do fine with
no alarm

But how can I defend my family against an enemy who doesn't exist?

Which is why this notion of a war on terror I humbly choose to resist

Let's say by chance that our "enemy" is truly a legitimate threat

I wonder, has the government made the right moves to deal with him
yet?

If the painful hard-hitting truth be told, I'd say that America's biggest
error

Was buying into this ridiculous notion that we're fighting in a War on
Terror

Social Security Swindle

Eating up my paycheck is this covetous cash monster
Systemized rip off run by cold rapacious mobsters
I'm bound to get busted for disobeying their requirements
Afraid of falling below the poverty line after my retirement
I'm supposed to trust these clowns to cover me in the future
When their trying to turn me into a penniless moocher
Going from place to place begging for money to pay-
The bills that I owe that are overpriced anyway
Don't I have the smarts to invest in what I desire?
Whether I invest in gold or become a multiple home buyer?
Get your hands out of my bank accounts! Don't touch my
    investments!
Your criminalized system needs more than a reassessment
It needs a deep hole with a tombstone that reads
"Death to this fraudulent deception rooted in greed"
A booming and vibrant economy can be rekindled
By first throwing out the Social Security Swindle!

The Department of Mental Strangulation

What need do we have for the government in our children's
    schooling?

Everything proposed by the common people they keep on overruling

These bureaucrats want to teach the kids reading, writing and
    artithmetic?

But when it comes to where our tax money goes, they can't even keep
    up with it

Keeping the children ignorant so they can grow into mindless slaves

Being drugged, then used up as future resources and tossed into the
    grave

Poor kids have no knowledge of our precious Bill of Rights

Conditioned to step on others to succeed and become money hungry
    sybarites

Filling them with all types of poison substances from Ritalin to Prozac

Let's cut to the chase and for a school treat give them Marijuana and
    Crack

We need a renewal of local control over what our children are learning

So let's stop bothering the government with ideas they plan to keep
    overturning

This government division is wasting space and squandering precious
    money

The joke played on the people was not, is not, nor ever will be funny

If we're going to have a country that enjoys a valid education

Then let's abolish the Department of Mental Strangulation

Much Stronger

So you don't have the time to rise and contend for American
    liberation?

But yet can endulge yourself in the freedoms achieved by the previous
    generation

How many excuses have you made for not wanting to fight?

Talking about your lack of time and how your money's too tight

When someone else is abused you claim you're not personally affected

Yet if they embraced the same sorry attitude toward you, I know you'd
    feel hurt and rejected

Thousands died in a Tsunami in Asia and Africa, you hardly blinked
    an eye

But the moment you can't eat your favorite meal you cuss, complain
    and cry

You have the audacity to poke fun at true patriots and freedom
    fighters?

While you mindlessly heed puppet politicians making hollow
    promises written by speech writers

Worst yet, you babble much about what can't be achieved

It's unfortunate that too much of your poison happens to be well
    received-

By those wanting to find the easy way out of an aggressive and grueling
    contest

Throwing up the lame classic smokescreen called "I gave it my best"

It's not my intention to make you a bloodthirsty warmonger

But if you changed your attitude and actions America could be much
    stronger.

Straighten Up and Get Right

In this day when selfishness sits supremely on the throne
Is it any wonder that many feel so isolated and alone?
Always talking about what can't be done for another
And how we have no room in our hearts to love a sister or a brother
Our communities have been destroyed, so the devil is celebrating
And coming up with more sinister ways to keep the family
    disintegrating
Drugs, gang warfare, poverty, abortion, absentee fathers and aids
Ravish our very children's lives and their youthfulness desperately
    fades
Searching the world for leaders and those who will bring liberation
We need to keep our eyes on the one who brings true salvation
Jesus is the black family's only hope, there can be no substitution
For the one who's bloodshed is precious and powerful enough to
    redeem this crippled institution
It is time to turn ourselves over to him through repentance and by
    surrender
To be forgiven by Him through His grace and mercy for we are all
    multiple offenders
So before we turn ourselves in for sleep in the darkest night
The Lord's message for the African-American family is simple:
    straighten up and get right

Further Decay

I often ponder where we're headed as a nation
Will we end up as other countries dying of starvation?
Could there be a coming crisis affecting our water supply?
That leaves us dehydrated with skin flaky and dry
When will the price of gas completely erode our savings?
It's bad enough that what we have now is merely shavings
Who'll pick up the pieces of America when it's totally ravaged?
I pray that our country's not left with immense irreparable damage
What will be the quality of our children's education?
Perhaps more washing of the brain or mental assassination
Can we afford to raise a family without plunging headfirst into debt?
I hear much about saving our wealth, but haven't seen much action yet
If we go into another war, will we obliterate the next generation?
Might as well since unto so many we're a barbaric civilization
Where will we go unless we repent in sorrow today?
Straight to the courtroom of judgment and thus further decay

Assignment Complete!

I must step up to the battlefield, because life is so short

This mission laid upon my heart, I refuse to abort

Making friends is secondary to doing God's will

No time for laying back and lounging by my cozy window sill

I resolve to stand against an abusive quasi-fascist regime

Committing swindles worse than those involved in ponzi schemes

If I am a man of God, I must manifest it in every way

Even in war if my very life is the price that I must pay-

To see justice in a land that's been robbed of all that's true and good

By forcing people to digest tyranny that tastes bitter as wormwood

The love I have for family and friends will be tried in the fire

Will I endure the fervent heat, or give in and simply expire?

Though death may take hold of me, before liberation is obtained

At least I'll die knowing the battle was worth every moment I strained

And when I enter that awesome heavenly paradise to sit at the Savior's feet

I'll be strengthened in His very presence knowing that my life's assignment is complete!

History's Next Great Revolution

Your mamma warned you about guys like me
Radical minded headstrong rebels fighting for liberty
She said I was nothing but a reckless danger
Which is why, when I came by she treated me like a stranger
The foul smelling garbage she poured into your mind
About not hooking up with and loving my particular kind
Was nothing more to me than a mere vexation
Diced and mixed with a couple of ounces of commonplace irritation
Ignorant of my heart's desire and moral intentions
I guess I can dig her bottled in self-centered apprehensions
Anyhow, baby doll join me in my fight for emancipation-
From mind bending and twisting controllers of media stations
Feeding us tainted pictures of reality to keep us in confinement
In the meantime, we need to strive for political dealignment
Stand by me darling, as I join the battle already in progress
While those who dog me out sit idly by and retrogress
It'll be worth your while loving a man who'll fight to the finish
Never allowing my hopes for justice and freedom to be diminished
So sweetheart, don't allow others to fill your destiny with pollution
And keep you from joining this man in history's next great revolution

That's My Guarantee!

I'm stepping onto the battlefield of my life's dreams
Reaching beyond the atmosphere into the deepest and darkest
    extremes
Drawing strength and courage from the God of the Bible
Knowing His power in me is critical to my very survival
Enemies surround me with desire to shed my blood
But I'll overwhelm them like a fierce and raging flood
I'll shoot out from the chamber like a turbo charged missile
Breaking up mountains yet remaining clear and sharp as a whistle
As the moment draws nigh to fulfill my life's call
I'll dig in firmly with my feet ready to charge right in and brawl
Staying on the offence is necessary for a total conquest
A truth which few comprehend, let alone are able to digest
I want to join the ranks of those faithful and dedicated-
To completing the work of their life, no matter how complicated
In closing out this rhyme, I'll make a simple decree
I will fight to the finish and that's my guarantee

Everyday is a Moment to Seize

I witness with my very eyes the wonder of creation
Whether I'm at home or cruisin' the country on my vacation
Auburn color tinted skies over the desert in the west
As I roll down the window feeling the heat move over my chest
I see the eight legged creature's crawl to their hiding place
Running fast from a shadow prancing along with such grace
Moving on to the heavy wooded land covering rivers and streams
Watching our brightest star reflect off the water by casting its glowing
  beams
I go on to the mountains which have a frigid chill above
Snow capped wonders of God's handiwork, yes I'm reminded of His
  love
Yes the mountains give me a glimpse of His majesty and power
But they also remind me that He's by my side when life goes sour
On my way back to my house, I reflect on all the wonderful sights-
Looked upon by my very eyes in the early morning and late night
I needed such an adventure to help set my over stressed mind at ease
And realize when it comes to living for God everyday is a moment to
  seize

Shut Up!

Quit lying to me about a four year degree
And about how obtaining one will set me free
Don't feed my ears with the same song and dance
About how following the rules will give me an advance-
In life to have the elaborate two story house
Packaged with a two car garage and lovely spouse
Four beautiful babies, a hamster, dog and cat
To keep the family company, and chase off the rats
I learned the hard way that the path to success
Is through learning of God's ways and how He chooses to bless
Not by racing with rats and going after molded cheese
Slaving away all of my years and being knocked to my knees
Looking back I see how much time has been wasted through
    believing-
That the dog-eat-dog mentality is necessary for achieving-
A fulfilling life that puts food on the table and juice in my cup
If you come to me with your lies again, I'll respectfully tell you to shut
    up!

Nice Try

Nice try Big Brother in trying to take me apart
Sending a gorgeous woman to win over my heart
Recognizing I'm a threat to your demented kingdom
Refusing to be a mindless bum in your occultic fiefdom
You send her my way with a smile so charming
Grace mingled with cuteness and beauty so disarming
Yes I admit I stumbled and fell for your trick
But as I fall I can recover with precision that's lightning quick
Reverse the grip she has on my emotions
Reaffirm my desire for battle and my devotion
To the very cause of true life and American liberation
While escaping your deceptive plan for my assassination
How low can you stoop in using her for your selfish gain
Paying her to break me down and cause my heart pain
Looks like I'm too resilient, plus God opened my eyes
To the foul game you were planning to ambush me by surprise

Ride Off Into the Sunset

I'm gonna buy myself a horse, perhaps a black stallion
Who knows one day I might head up a strong battalion
Anyhow about my horse, I'll build him a cool stable
Custom made with the finest of wood and a finely built water table
He'll get the best that his owner can possibly buy
Good nutrition and exercise to keep him strong and spry
As he grows his coat will shine as the wind blows through his mane
I'll guide him through his growing up by taking hold of his reins
He will be the strongest horse that has ever walked on land
Having all the cute little mares under his caring hand
My stallion and I will ride many hours together
Doesn't matter if it's sunny or in inclement weather
Perhaps he'll carry me and my future bride to our honeymoon site
Then he'll wait outside while me and my lady have ourselves a good
    night
But we haven't quite reached that point in my life just yet
So just for a brief while me and my horse will ride off into the sunset

You Will Be Slain!

Look here New World Order I know your crooked policies
Play a major role in all of the worldwide atrocities
But let me make this clear while the floor is wide open
I refuse to let you ruin my life keeping me in the dark and gropin'-
For a life line squandering my years away merely trying to survive
While you and your boys sit around with evil plans to contrive
What's on your agenda, another world war or perhaps a tsunami?
Giving Americans another reason to blame the lame Commies
Just because you're a reprobate doesn't give you license to wreck others
I'd pack you on a shuttle and ship you to Planet X if I had my druthers
Then that way you'd be right at home being able to do as you please
Rather than hurting innocent humans you'd die of your own disease
What a relief it'd be to get rid of you and the evil for which your stand
That desires nothing more than to ruin my very homeland
And all that people living here have worked so hard to obtain
I am as clear as crystal when I say that "you will be slain!"

A Compelling Reason to Fight

When I see those pretty little eyes warming my very soul
I must admit ever sheepishly that it's my heart that you stole
For when I had my sights set on battling the Illuminati
You crept up silently and yes little girl I do confess that you got me
Coiled yourself tightly around my heart chambers
Scared me momentarily I felt I was in danger
Of losing you to some hurt or harm then I realized-
Protecting you is all the more reason to fight, you're so tender in my
    eyes
Then I regained my bearings and put this picture in a frame
My heart being won over by you is no reason to be ashamed
In fact I'm inspired to fight even harder against evil globalism
Desiring to protect you and your generation from wicked terrorism
I think of your precious beauty and how it warms me inside
Then I get a rushing surge of strength in my posture and my stride
Set my stance determined to battle for you from this evening until
    daylight
Your precious sweetness stirs me up giving me a compelling reason to
    fight

Jeffrey Alexander Hamilton

Before They Drive Us Underground

They've built a fortress around our nation
Subjecting us to fear and cold hearted degradation
Implanting our kids with microchips, colored wires on their brains
Keeping us under surveillance locking young men in chains
Poisonous vaccinations causing cerebral disabilities
Impairing rational judgment and hindering cognitive abilities
Forcing us to accept their methods of formal learning
Claiming it'll help us all achieve more efficient earnings
Our atmosphere is ravaged giving us crude weather
They use chemical attacks hoping to destroy all of us together
Genetically enhanced nutrition eating away our insides
I see it as part of their wicked plan for mass genocide
Will We the People open our eyes before it's too late?
Or are we too far under the grand umbrella of a cruel fate?
I'd like to think that we can turn this mess around
Before the Global Elite succeed in driving us underground

Crushed, Bruised and Swollen

I've had my heart crushed by foul circumstances
Broken dreams, delayed hopes and failed romances
Been kicked when I was down bloodied and battered
Felt the pain in my soul when my whole world shattered
Laughed at and criticized, rumors spread about me
By namby-pamby milk toast punks who can't clearly see
I'm on fire and if they happen to be curious
They can step right up and know I'm fervently furious-
With being walked on by my soul's bitter rival
In my heart I hear the message that it's time for revival
I'm on the comeback with prayer and fighting
In a lifelong battle that's dangerous and exciting
All my enemies will start falling like dominoes
Eating my fist like candy and digesting my deathblows
Then through God's provision I'll take back what was stolen
While my opposition is left crushed, bruised and swollen

You May End Up Dead!

Do you earnestly wish to bring out the Lion in me?
I feel as if you have no clue how vicious I can be
Yes you see me calmly going about my day
Smiling pleasantly at everyone who passes my way
But don't think my fury won't reach the surface
Blasting out molten rocks making you criminals nervous
My indignation is ignited by the hurt you've caused children
You bunch of reprobate minded cold hearted villains
Putting poison in their vaccination wrecking their brains
Creating a criminal minded nation of the walking insane
Then you subject them to mindless entertainment
Leading them to inevitable bondage and enchainment
After that you have the nerve to forcibly test them psychologically
When you've already sentenced them to death biologically
Keep this in mind, if you want to keep your head
Stay away from these children or you may end up dead!

This Man of God Has Spoken

I'm in a dogfight for my survival
Kicking in the teeth of my demented rivals
Breaking off the chains of the Illuminati
Cut loose from the shackles when they swore they got me
I'm enraged, a rolling ball of fury
The verdict is in I've got word from the jury
I'm guilty for having too much passion and fire
Ignited by God and my heartfelt desires
I will press until my limbs are weary
Don't take it personal if I don't look too cheery
I'm locked in a contest bruised, battered and tired
Calling on the Lord Jesus to keep me inspired
To fight against this malignant New World disorder
Defending my family, friends and our national border
The fatal plans of my enemies will be broken
Take heed you crooks for this man of God has spoken

Jeffrey Alexander Hamilton

Just What it Deserves

I see my great country sinking down into quicksand
Through manipulated currency and a few evil hands
The Federal Reserve system is a beast untamed
Leaving American people financially broke and lame
Why must I work two jobs just to breathe air?
Keeping my head barely above water, it just ain't fair
1913 was the year our nation was secretly molested
I wish more people knew the truth, stood up and protested
Perhaps we wouldn't have to face this hideous monster
While being controlled and sold out by cold hearted mobsters
Robotic officials come on television saying they know what's best
By telling us who to vote for and how to spend, save and invest
At the same time very few of them will face the reality
That the common man has suffered monetary brutality
At the hands of the reckless and vicious Federal Reserve
It's past time this money mafia gets just what it deserves!

It Must Start With Me

I can't leave this earth without making a way for the young
Living one way but speaking the opposite with my tongue
My pilgrimage in this world is my one opportunity
To promote God's love and a sense of family community
Unifying different races to fight against global slavery
No time for cowardice, but there's always room for bravery
This war will be fought hard with every ounce of my energy
Along with other fellow Americans forming an awesome synergy
To tear down the dome of evil and wicked oppression
With hope and determination not to repeat the Great Depression
No more wars for profit filling the pockets of the Elite
While they force every working person to lick the dust off their feet
Looking at the beautiful children that I pass by everyday
My heart compels me to obey God in making a better way-
For the pillars of the future to live in a world that's free
If I desire a stronger America for my children, then it must start with
   me

Mind Pollution

Everywhere men turn it seems like we're bombarded
With images of naked women to be stared upon and discarded
The physical form of a female is highly enticing
Taking the coldest man through the process of deicing
Setting him aflame in a blazing hot furnace of lustful desire
Ten times the fervency of the most aggressively scorching wildfire
What's a boy to think of women at the youthful age of ten?
When all that's placed before Him is a few threads covering skin
Pornography grips a man by the throat forcing him into submission
Causing him to lose his grip on reality and sensible cognition
Hunger pangs of lust are never fully and completely satisfied
Reaching and taking more to fill an empty space, and still not gratified
Now he cannot look at a woman as a person of godly worth
Smiled upon and regarded as delightful from the day of her birth
Imprisoned and ruled by an evil and mind altering deceptive allusion-
That porn is beautiful, when in reality it's nothing but mind pollution

How I Starved the Cash Monster

I've got my sword and bow with many arrows in my quiver
I also have a certified package of pain to deliver
To the first one on my hit list who is a cold hideous beast
Who broke into my bank account and had himself a feast
Left me in a river of debt flowing over my head
Trying to drown me and take me under leaving me for dead
Thank God I made it safely to the surface
Swam to the shore, now I'm going to light my furnace
The first to go is that bondage called plastic
Some say I'm overdoing it, bordering on the drastic
Next thing for me is to cut down on consumption
Build my fortitudinal muscle, going forward with gumption
I think now it's time for me to bust my rump and produce-
From my God given talents and take time to reduce-
The portions of currency I'm feeding this foul creature
"How I Starved the Cash Monster" will be the title of my feature

Completely Healed

Right at this time I'm beat down and disgusted
My head is pounding my heart has been busted
I've battled furiously to set everything in place
Only to see it all blow right up in my face
How many blows must I take before my hope expires
My situation seems bleak as does my passionate fire
My soul is in the iron hot vice of persecution
I'll pray till my tongue is tired from begging a solution
To fixing this madness that keeps me in prison
Lord I need your strength and a brand new vision
Enough is enough of this spiraling madness
Trying to lay me flat and lock me into sadness
I'm through with the pitiful, tired and lame excuses
That I lay on myself along with reckless abuses-
Thrown at the man who I see in my reflection
It's time for a new resolve and a positive direction
The past is gone and dead committed to the dust
My present is hopeful in my God I fully trust
Though my pain is manifested in these words I've revealed
It won't abide because through God I'm completely healed

The Fraudulent Joke

Now it's time to talk more about a cold reality
Run by stone hearts with a mob mentality
Every year they cause the people unfair trauma
Playing the cold villain in this warfare drama
Stealing our money that we slave so hard for
Take away our goods then turn around and cry for more!
Why should we live fearfully in the land of the free?
Living under the chains of an ungodly decree
That wars against the livelihood of American people
Through laws that are confounding and downright deceitful
We need a tax system that will replenish our nation
Not one that's wrought with tyranny and aggravation
One where We the People will be happy to play our role
In helping our country to be healthy, strong and whole
So that all can find true freedom in our monetary complex
Where we're are not treated as financially fraudulent suspects
Then we can own houses with food in the cabinet
And provide for our friends when their funds are inadequate
Living in a land that's free from the cumbersome yoke—
Of the Internal Revenue Disservice, a.k.a the fraudulent joke

Jeffrey Alexander Hamilton

Unpatriotic Act

Now the government has found another foul reason
To harass the innocent in and out of season
By expanding the definition of being a criminal
Under the phony guise of American principle
Claiming such an act will protect the nation
From terrorist thugs headed for damnation
Yet in reality all Americans are suspects
From the high paid yuppies to the social rejects
Lest any of us should get a little too cozy-
In our easy chairs thinking American life is rosy
We must keep in mind that this act is an invasion
Upon our sovereignty, so we must rise to the occasion
And throw out such an evil invading our states
Because the government has opened up the floodgates
To drown We the People in this brutal legislation
This unpatriotic act is deserving of condemnation

In Greater Measure

I'm gonna share a little bit of my philosophy
About big business taking people's property
Doesn't the Bible command us not to cheat and steal
Through force or by manipulating business deals
Taking the homes of those working sixty hours
To live their dream now their hope is going sour
Bullied and forced into making a life changing decision
Hanging by a thread and getting very little provision
Instead they're given change fit for chumps
Who plunder the poor while they sit on their rumps
Collecting loads of money to attain more control
While the average American man is thrown into a pesthole-
That's infested by the disease of greed, which makes the poor man sick
While big business men get fatter and their pocket's grow thick
It's time for America to defend it's precious land
Against this sweeping evil that carries a heavy hand
Breaking down the elderly who have no place to go
They are to be honored but they get treated as the foe-
Who stand in the way of Big Business' global sweep
What these heartless pirates sow, in greater measure they will reap

Fighting the New World Order

Every moment that we rise we need to pray
For wisdom and courage to fight everyday
We're in need of a nationwide revival
It's time to repent and trust the God of the Bible
Oh yeah there's more to the solution
Learn the Bill of Rights and Constitution
Give ourselves, family and friends an education
About the current global empire and its manipulation
That's taking lives while robbing others of prosperity
Disguised in a cloak of loving sincerity
We need to write our representatives in office
If they don't hear us, then we'll render them jobless
Reach out to fellow neighbors on our block
What we share with them may come as a shock
But they've got to know about this information
Not more political rhetoric to give their party validation
Let's be a pillar of strength in our community
I don't mean to be so trite but we're in dire need of unity
As danger continues to cross into our borders
We need to take these steps in fighting the New World Order

Deadly Tap Water

H2O is essential to my survival
Giving My dehydrated body a cool revival
I can't poison my system with harsh metal
Which I try to boil away in my tea kettle
Who knows of the mess I ingest into my system?
Killing my organs and disrupting my body's rhythm
The New World thugs want to harm the population
Leading us into sluggishness and mental stagnation
The hurt they desire for us should come to no surprise
Leading to deadly poison and chemical highs
The excessive flouride is killing our brains
Making us more docile and quasi-insane
I'm leading a movement against this quiet assassination
That's a secret war against the people of this nation
Coming through the faucet is the deadly tap water
A fatal weapon leading us all to the slaughter

Jeffrey Alexander Hamilton

We Keep On Counting

Think with me for a moment about your precious baby
Now picture him or her being held by your lady
Smiling brightly a picture perfect view of God's creation
Second only to the Lord, they're the object of your admiration
Now get this, all of a sudden they're robbed and assaulted
Bulldozed by tyrants, steamrolled and asphalted
Rendered as bits and pieces to be walked on by the Elite
Regarded as nothing more than being trampled by their feet
Beheaded, blown up for a crime of which they're innocent
And spoken of as if they're animals by the cold hearted and insolent
Imagine the pain that would tear upon your very heart
Wrenching your guts beyond pain's threshold and ripping them apart
You take hold of the head of your baby in your hand
But there is little you can do because the enemy has invaded your land
Death of the precious children around you is steadily mounting
Well that's life for millions of Iraq's whose deaths we keep on counting

How Many Soldiers?

Alright I'm angry about the soldiers slain
In a war driven by evil imperialistic gain
It's too bad that our society is so unenlightened
Complacent in our mind set while tyranny is heightened
Knowing young teens with much potential we won't see anymore
All because they were the bait in this unlawful war
What will the extent of our judgment be?
Upon a people with plenty of light but who refuse to see
I have a heart to defend my land against danger from abroad
But I'm not wasting my life in a war that's a fraud
At the rate we're going we'll have no military left-
To fight legitimate battles not based upon lies and theft
America please let's wake up before our youth are gone
Buried in graves custom made by those elitist running the Pentagon
The movement against sovereign invasion is quite a burden to
  shoulder
But I'll carry that burden if I can help spare the life of a soldier

Jeffrey Alexander Hamilton

Sears Tower

Lately I've had a taste in my mouth kind of sour
With fears that our Government will hit the Sears Tower
Why not? It stands boldly as an American wonder
Its destruction will come crashing down sounding like thunder
Panic will hit the streets worst than any financial crisis
Prompted by the Elite who want to render us lifeless
To those in the Windy City please keep your eyes peeled
More carefully than those tiptoeing through a volatile minefield
Something smells fishy and it's not coming from the Great lake
But from an evil maniacal plan to make Chicago shake-
From fear and terror and from the actual rumblings
Of a monstrous building that might take a down tumbling
There are few times that I hope that I'm wrong
So here's one of those few, but we have to stay strong
And resist the Tyranny invading our home cities and towns
New York was bad enough, we can't let the Sears Tower go down

London 911

"Not again" I said to myself as I read the morning paper
Bringing back memories of demolished skyscrapers-
Right here in America such a heart wrenching reality
Reminding us that life on earth can have a cruel finality
London has been hit, the innocent killed once again
We need to prosecute those guilty for this sin
Will we just let them get away with causing more death and fear?
And be docile like simple sheep getting ready for the shears
This madness can't continue to spread around the globe
Murdering people for power and leaving nations disrobed
The pop media lies covering the ones who stand to gain
From spreading terror and bringing sorrow and shame-
To lives everywhere regardless of nationality
The moment is now to embrace the reality-
That the UK's been hit hard far beyond an emergency
We need to fight back with a focused sense of urgency

Border Stand!

While the media has our minds twisted in propagandist lies
There's a war on the border that may open some eyes
Over six hundred dead on both sides, cops and civilians
In a fight over drugs bringing the country billions
Once again our Government moves the chess pieces
Many innocent slain and the fear steadily increases
Cars bombed, people burned right in the heart of Texas
America's been busted right in the solar plexus
The pain is severe we're struggling for our very breath
Trying to defend our country or what little is left
Why hasn't there been an outcry bout' the border madness
Leaving families broken covered in a cloud of sadness
Police officers are killed and the news won't report
Because the Elite has their hands in the highest court
I guess We the People have to take up some arms
To keep these commandos from doing our people more harm

Abortion

Slain in the womb are the babies of my generation
Torn from limb to limb in the time of their gestation
These inestimable lives never embraced the light of birth
Discarded as mere matter and devalued in their worth
This slaughter continues today as a mad ritual
Some are repeat offenders, in their case it's habitual
Killing these babies is murder why don't we realize?
Can we even imagine the horror of their cries?
As they get poked and jabbed leaving a hole in their brain
Sucking out cerebral tissue what an incomprehensible pain!
These priceless creations of God aren't immune to affliction
Slaying the innocent has been a bloodthirsty addiction-
For this nation who has yet to stop all the killings
We'd better wake up now or our judgment will be awfully chilling
God is calling for repentance in how we regard and value life
So we can realize the wrong in cutting a precious baby with a knife

Jeffrey Alexander Hamilton

Weapons of Mass Seduction

Once again we've been lured into believing a lie
All because of our criminal Government's cry
About the need to undercover weapons so deadly
That eat away at people killing them slowly and steadily
The fists started pumping, the groupthink in place
To prompt the Americans to get behind this race
That has the aim to conquer sovereign nations
Starting with Iraq and extending its evil plantation
All across the world making a sordid empire
So those at the top can be worshiped and be addressed as "Sire"
Anyway back to my point we've been conned again
Parading around the globe like cold hearted hit-men
Quickly filling in the blanks of our justification-
For ravaging people's lands and getting mindless acclamation-
From those who don't know better, who are mere followers
When it comes to thinking they are simply borrowers-
Of a mind set carved out for them so they won't have to think
And realize this ungodly war has more than just one kink
The Globalists have already begun their population reduction
By killing our sound minds and luring us in with weapons of mass
seduction

Lunacy in Our Souls

I love and admire the strength and beauty of a woman's grace
Which is why I believe it should be kept in the right place
I've come to realize that we've gone out of our minds
By insisting that women be in battle on the front line
Serving in uniform is one thing if that's the place she chooses
But I can't stand for women being subjected to harsh abuses
In the event that she's captured and held in chains by the nemesis
I'm afraid my message isn't heard so I say this with emphasis-
She's not made for battling with men in the thickest conflict
Going toe to toe with cold blooded killers and national convicts
Her mind can be used in other realms of our forces
I know I'm going against what Radical Feminism endorses
There's always the exception the one who's big tough and strong
But we can't make her the rule which such an ideology stands upon
Women aren't equipped for fighting on the battle front
This is hard to accept for some but at times I must be blunt
Why let our sisters and daughters be torn to bits and pieces?
It's hard enough losing brothers, sons and nephews, now they want
    our nieces!
Common sense should tell us that men and women have differing
    roles
If we put women on the front line then we've embraced lunacy in our
    souls

Jeffrey Alexander Hamilton

Land of the Free and Pure

In our brave land a tumor has developed
Spreading so rapidly the whole nation has been enveloped
It's caused much fear and weakened our immunity
Stirred up hopelessness and doubt bringing about disunity
This very disease is in need of swift destruction
Not more time to due harm or rapid reproduction
While we sleep many people are being slain
It's peccant to stand by watching people die in vain
Let's grab the knife of the Constitution
And come together with a newfound resolution
That we're going to terminate the cancer in our land
We the People have to take matters into our hands
With the blessing of God we can beat this malady
That steps on our backs behaving so callously
The Neocon cancer must go, our land is in need of a cure
So we can once again be the land of the free and pure

A Price to Pay

Who really is behind all of these child abductions?
I realize that over time kidnaping's have gone on a reduction
Nevertheless I'm still concerned about the truth of these events
Blanketed by mass media keeping us in deep suspense
Devil worship is real and the stories are so horrific
About little ones being tortured and induced by pills that are soporific
Molested and beaten in ways that I can hardly mention-
By those whose souls are in a state of moral tension
Why is the truth being hidden? Is there a Luciferian agenda?
The evidence has been revealed now we have quite a dilemma
Will we let the legacy of those young children be disregarded?
While allowing the ones we're still blessed to have remain unguarded?
God is angry on behalf of the children who have died
While being mangled as they screamed out and cried
I'm on the hunt for justice to rectify the families of the satanically
    sacrificed
It's not a duty for me but a just privilege before Christ
If anyone comes near my child with thoughts of torturing them in
    mind
I'll justifiably get rough and put them on their very behind
Enough of Satan killing kids and having his way
We either end this madness now or we'll have a price to pay!

United Nations

As Americans we're strong enough on our own
So to the United Nations please leave us alone
We don't need to be caught up into your mess
Our sovereignty is precious we need no more stress
It's bad enough our nation is falling to pieces
You tend to get stronger as our strength decreases
Perhaps if you were legitimate it would be another story
But it seems as if your conduct is rather gross and gory
Perversion has eroded your solid reputation
Hurting little children while aiding in globalization
Bribing little girls with candy so you can get them in bed
You're in need of prayer, there's something wrong with your head
The good you may have done acts as only a cover-
Of your attempts to make five year old girls your lovers
Once again get out! We don't need your evil policies
Nor do we want any part of your national atrocities

Brain Microwave

In this modern day with all the fancy technology
I have a word to speak without any apology
Big Brother keeps a tracking device on his slaves
With something I'll call the brain microwave
Every day we carry them making our calls
Teens flaunt them hanging out with friends at the malls
The radiation oven in my kitchen is bad enough
No need to have it pressed against my head like earmuffs
Another thing, these little toys can cause ocular damage
An additional tool our slave masters can use to their advantage-
In schooling us, ruling us, stepping on, beating up and ridiculing us
And when we're fried up and dried up we can't speak up and raise a
    fuss
The cell phone may be convenient but we need to think twice
Are we people or laboratory rats, monkeys and mice
It's time to find a way to communicate while preserving our brains
Without a mental microwave to drive us insane

Simply Forgive

In this battle against mobsters and criminal minded thugs
I'm not for being lovely dovey and giving out hugs
On the other hand I must live free from binding hatred
I want to fulfill my destiny not letting my time be wasted
Though I jump into the battle wanting to strike my nemesis
I must remember everyone's entitled to a second genesis
I'll pray for my enemy to wake up and see the light
So he'll recognize that the harm he's doing to others isn't right
I'm not giving him a pass for the atrocities he's committing
But I'm following my God to whom I must be submitting-
Day in and day out as I stand in the gap and do battle-
Against a foe so cunningly clever and not easily rattled
It's the sin that I hate not so much the individual
Who's caught up and taking part in satanic rituals
I cannot forget that in order for me to fully live
I must fight the NWO while taking the time to simply forgive

So Lazy

These gas prices are straight up out of control
Big Money's laughing at us while fattening his bankroll
Crude oil has increased in dollars per barrel
In a time of bankruptcy and national financial peril
Inflation is the name of the game in this global monopoly
Haphazard misuse of our money managed so sloppily
I say those of us who drive should gather our gas receipts
Send them to the White House and Congressman's luxury suites
Demanding a significant portion of our money back
And not give in to their choreographed yakety-yak
In a time when people can barely pay their house note or rent
We can't allow our funds to be casually misspent
How about this? Let's all try a new course
Every family in America buy a family horse
And when the auto industry starts losing money and going crazy
Perhaps Washington will hear us and stop being so lazy

Wake Up Church!

Church of God please open your eyes
Don't buy into the Governments lies
They have so many evil plans in store
Beginning with a series of Middle Eastern wars
Using phony terror as a means to justify—
Filling up their military roster that's in short supply
Have we been so dumbed down and blinded
That we like lost lambs follow the reprobate minded
The Lord is warning us not to be deceived
And to trust the leading of the Holy Spirit we received-
On the day we gave our lives to Jesus Christ
We must follow Him regardless of the price
Perhaps it will cost us our very life's breath
When we stand strong in our contemporary culture of death
Let's not be soft in this age of ease and modernity
After all, this life is short, but long is the stretch of eternity

A Cowardly New World

The Elite seek to control the entire population
Through mind control and medical manipulation
Using those who resist their tyranny as clay pigeons
They desire to create an evil one world religion
A nation of cyborgs is their mission and aim
We're no more than checkers in their global game
I see in the schools how freedom of speech is scorned
People of the world, please be forewarned
This new world designed to keep us safe from harm
Is all the more reason for us to sound the alarm
Shaking up the idle, waking up those who slumber
Before they get tagged and labeled with a serial number
We are five minutes from the midnight hour
As we witness our dreams of liberty go sour
A revolution is the necessary means of being free
We must kneel before God and earnestly plea
That He will strengthen and preserve our minds
So that we can fight and defend mankind-
Against this cowardly new world that's being created
By those whose evil mind sets are dilapidated

Being Desensitized

There is a disease I pray to resist with all of my energy
One which deserves to looked upon contemptibly
The Illuminati puppet masters work behind the scenes
Stirring up conflicts that don't amount to a hill of beans
The daily news is filled with the same ole' mess
About who slept with who and what's the latest dress
You can't tell me that such nonsense is truly valid
Anymore than what's the best dressing for my salad
We're told that inflation is just by happenstance
And we the people nod yes like we're in a trance
I find myself sometimes slipping into a docile mind set
That's easily manipulated to be of no threat-
To the mind controlling power hungry Global Elite
Who want the whole population bowing at their feet
I can't be slack I must be vigilant, it's time I realized
The urgent need to ward off the disease of being desensitized

The Capture of Saddam Hussein

What am I to think about the capture of Hussein?
The man who apparently caused so many Iraqi's pain
The so called threat to our nation's livelihood and safety
His acts of evil dictatorship are often spoken of vaguely
I'm not a fan or supporter him, in fact think he's a criminal
I'd be too nice in saying that he's a well rounded imbecile
But there's more to the story that's rarely reported
With a couple ounces of truth that's madly distorted
How did America benefit by the capture of this man?
Isn't he a major player in our government's plan?
An asset of the CIA, an actor in a major production
Set upon a stage to act with rage and pose as an obstruction-
To the people who desire to live free from a stiff-neck tyrant
So when he sets the world aflame the US brings a hydrant-
In order to extinguish the fire that he was told to set ablaze
The truth about Saddam's legitimate capture once had me in a haze
But as I began to look much deeper the evidence became so clear
That the Government falsified another story to feed into my ear
Saddam is nothing more than a tool in the hand of our modern regime
Thus his capture is only a minuscule part of the Governments evil
  scheme

You'd Better Not Touch My Baby Girl!

I know your desire for world conquest is written in a document
When it comes to possessing the Earth you want to be the sole occupant
To attain a new century made in your image you will maim and kill to achieve
The fact that you would actually follow through is not at all hard to believe
With soldier's being cut short of life you're in need of a new supply
To carry out your colonialistic plans while military casualties multiply
So you're looking into a draft or shall I correctly say armed forces conscription
Where you've really lost your mind is when you say girls can fit the description-
Of a front line soldier armed for battle ready to slay the mighty foe
Such a thought of complete insanity wasn't even thought of years ago
The bloodiest of battles is a man's domain if you haven't yet realized
So putting a woman in his place will get her thoroughly pulverized
That brings me to the main point of this expression so true from my heart
I won't sit idly by and let you tear the American family apart
You've killed my brother, father, uncle and you tried to take my son
But you have the audacity to try take my girl, we'll you'll be staring into my gun
My little princess? The one who I hold so closely in my arms
Knows that she can come to daddy whenever anyone does her harm
Be it a street thug, racist punk, rogue soldier or government pawn
If any one of them ever caused her pain they'd be spread all across my lawn
When I see those beautiful baby browns looking my way
I'm reminded that the Lord will care for her if I should soon pass away

So to all you global minded, imperialistic clowns you'd better not even bother

To send a notice of compulsory military service to this man's daughter

As I said before I will fight with every ounce of life that I possess

To keep her free from your chess game even if it means me taking one in the chest

From the day she emerged from momma's womb she touched my very core

So I say that God's precious gift to us will not be sacrificed in any unjust war

Seeing her walk, hearing her first words and feeling dynamite when she said "daddy"

I knew that I would pound the man who would ever treat her badly

I got long-winded in my explanation, but she's my only little doll in this cruel world

I'm sure my message is clear, but to sum it all up you'd better not touch my baby girl!

Lord Please Deputize Me

There's a battle for humanity and all that's sacred
Against an evil empire that's full of guile and hatred
Black, White, Asian, Pacific Islanders and Hispanics
All are bound to be doomed by this worldwide panic
That seeks to rob us leaving us beaten down and poor
They'll steal our last penny and still come for more
A pandemic disease is on their list of wicked plans
With a desire to annihilate the Americans and Afghans
They've taken hold of our money and our entertainment
They should be shipped to an island of total containment
That way we won't have to stand for their absurdity
Acting like they're a part of old world Nazi Germany
I'm ready for a rumble I am set on fighting back
Hoping to defend my country against this all out attack-
Coming from the Global Elite and their sorry minions
Lord please deputize me to war under your dominion

Let's Stand United

My hearts dream is that Americans will ban together
To route out the evil that's much worse than foul weather
It's time to quit having disputes between the races
And battle against the evil laughing in all of our faces
Your child is my concern, so please love mine too
Working side by side, we're bound to pull through-
Any barrier in our way set up by the adversary
Before we get started here's a little cautionary
This battle will demand every ounce of our might
So in the thickest of contests we mustn't lose sight-
Of the mighty God who's the sole source of our power
Giving us the edge when the enemy seeks to devour-
All that we've fought, bled and darn near died for
We'll let the Devil know we won't take anymore-
Of his barriers and lies that keep us divided
If we're true Americans, then let's stand united!

Jeffrey Alexander Hamilton

The Capital of Lies

Why should we believe anything that you say?
When you stand to gain from our society's decay
From Pearl Harbor to Northwoods on to the USS Liberty
You speak to us as if we're lost in utter stupidity
Vietnam was bad enough with many lives destroyed
It's the hard questions from the people that you choose to avoid
Such as what happened on Nine Eleven? Who stood to gain?
How will you all provide for the families in pain?
Where is Osama hiding? That man of terrorist fame
How did you really know where to locate Saddam Hussein?
Your elections are staged with your handpicked candidates
Playing games with our country that lies in dire straits
You control the media and the messages they speak
Even kids in first grade are hip to your dishonest techniques-
Used to attempt to keep the blinders over our eyes
When I think of Washington, I think of the capital of lies

Life Today

All people deserve a chance to live
With chance to receive and chance to give
A place to live a useful life
Money for a man and his wife
To raise their kids and build a house
As long as their good life allows-
Them to walk upon this earth
Let's celebrate the joy of birth
When children first learn to walk-
We'll clap our hands when they talk-
We'll change their diapers when they wet
And help them speak the alphabet
We must teach them of the Lord
And how to wield his righteous sword
There's a message I want to relay
Let's rejoice that we have life today

Military Dreams Shattered

I once considered service in the military before
Excited to see what such an adventure had in store
An opportunity to explore different nations
And to have my share of paid vacations
Now that I look back I see that the Great Divine
Kept me from signing my name on the line
It disgusts me to see what Washington has done
To America's vibrant daughters and sons
Placing them in wars that appear to be never-ending
The Government continues with its overspending
Poisoning the troops with toxic chemicals
While prompting them to shock detainees genitals
It would have been honorable to serve with distinction
But our military integrity is bound for extinction
Thanks to the Elite who have our armed forces tattered
Perhaps it's okay that my military dreams were shattered

White Slavery

Men of the world it's time to fight bravely
Against a perverted evil called White Slavery
Women and children sold into prostitution
It's time we tear down this wicked institution
Be vigilant and watch who's lurking on our streets
These predators are on the prowl looking for meat
We can't let our girls drift from our protection
Let us guard them with all of our strength and affection
That means going out of our way when we're tired—
To give them attention that is strongly desired
Taking them out shopping, then for a nice dinner
Teaching them how to grow into a solid winner
So they won't look to try and fill that desolation
With a stranger hunting for girls in isolation
I'm not fearmongering but we need to be aware-
Of a foul threat endangering those for whom we care

American Dream

I'm going to build myself a farm with of range for my cattle

Close to a river of pure water where I can take a boat and paddle

Get some good fish that I can take to my place, season up and cook

Being happy that the food I'm about to eat was caught on my hook

Maybe I'll get some chickens and a couple of horses for riding on the trail

Have a few pigs with a cat and dog to keep an eye on the duck and cottontail

There will be fresh air for my family, plenty of room for the kids to play

A spacious house with a cool set up if my friends need a place to stay

I'll need a pad in the city as well, for when I'm craving a vibrant pace of life

Yet I'll be able to retreat to my farm when I need relief from city strife

I know I may be fantasizing about a life so awesome and grand

But without a passion to follow, I have no foundation upon which to stand

The Lord has richly blessed me with a mind to follow my vision

A view of a world where all people can pursue and fulfill their life's mission

To be able to live as one desires is not a notion that's too crazy and extreme

In fact it's a foundational block to the structure of living the American dream

I'll Give You a Black Eye!

No more Big Brother watching me
Worrying about where I'm supposed to be
Having his camera right up in my face
I think I need to put this fool in his place
He knows all the numbers of my bank account
Tracking my expenses and every amount-
That I spend, that I give to those who are broke
Even knowing where I hang out with my kinfolk
I'm tired of living on his evil plantation
A rebellion is needed by my current generation
I won't run and hide, I'll be on the front line
Join me in showing Big Brother the stop sign
Telling him I don't need him as my care giver
He'd better take heed to the message I deliver
His days are numbered I'm telling him goodbye
Back off Big brother or I'll give you a black eye!

After the Dust Settles

Too many children are hurt by vaccinations
As they're forced to fit into educational plantations
Now some are like zombies with no emotion
Through being shot up with this mercury potion
It's a sad situation when I'm walking the halls
Seeing little boys staring blankly at the walls
You call their name but they don't respond
Their future is robbed, the parents have been conned
Into thinking that such poison would protect their child
Even the teachers have been horrendously beguiled-
Believing the foul nonsense coming from D.C.
It's in this hour that we must open our eyes and see-
The hurt, harm and damage done to our children
If we continue to allow this crap, then we're the true villain
Wrecking the future of our young with toxic metals
This danger will be clearly seen after the dust settles

Crying to His Mother

I'm tired of being watched day in and day out
By cold eyes staring leaving me in doubt-
As to whether I can trust this police state or not
That has my stomach tied up in a knot-
Wondering if they will take my family away?
To a gulag style camp and watch them decay
They know how much I spent on burgers and fries
Through their computerized network of crooked spies
In the form of small chips placed under my skin
I feel my heart throbbing from this cycle of sin
A scan to my retina to bring up my identity
I'm crying foul in this high tech century?
Why does Big Brother need my information?
Tracking me at home and on my vacation
He'd better be aware of the man he's stalking
One who's serious and not merely talking-
About the war of education I'm about to launch
No time for petty quarrels or sitting on my haunch
I have some plans up my sleeve for Big Brother
That'll send him home crying to his mother

Jeffrey Alexander Hamilton

I've Got to Keep My Cool

I've got to keep my cool in this day and age
When cops are bound to act out in rage
And club me for simply standing my ground
As I proclaim that I won't be pushed around-
Letting my family and friends be abused
While children are raped, drugged and misused-
For pleasure in an industry that's completely insane
Perverting God's gift of sex, putting kids to shame
My anger boils deep down inside my gut
Sometimes I wake up bleeding as if I've been cut
In reality it's nothing but sweat from my irateness
Which must be mixed with an ounce of sedateness
I must remain rational in fighting the opposition
Asking God's direction in fulfilling my mission
The battle at hand requires my full attention
But I must be cool and not fall out of contention

America's Economic Disgrace

Economic disaster the gas is too high
My income is falling like rain from the sky
Car notes are the price of a small apartment
My living in confined to a tiny compartment-
Tucked into the corner of a beautiful city
It's time that I start an economic committee
To try and figure out a new plan for the nation
Where all can live good with a bit of determination-
Working hard and smart to reap good crops
Not through minimum wage slave shops
Forget communism with all of its helotry
Restricting the child as well as the elderly
When one man is free it starts a chain reaction
Leading to liberation and soul satisfaction
That all of mankind can fully embrace
I'm crusading to end America's economic disgrace

Running Out of Time!

These last couple of days my head's been throbbing
From all the loud cheering with craniums vertically bobbing
Hailing the thief for creating more destruction
Our criminal Government's in need of mass reduction
Toss away FEMA with all their foul activity
Dump all the alphabet agencies in a river never to be-
Seen again, forget CNN, no more smiling a greedy grin
Maybe America can be free and delivered from sin
Not the model of perfection, but somewhat lawful
Over the last few decades, the Fed has been awful
We're always broke, the debt continues to mount
What's the problem can't these monetary agents count?
Anyway enough rambling about cash troubles
If I make one silly mistake suddenly my debt doubles
Anyhow I'm closing out the remainder of this rhyme
America is in trouble and we're running out of time!

Phony Patriots

Here we are with America going straight to hell
Meanwhile your priority is making your pockets swell
Taking in cash from those searching for truth
Robbing the retiree, family man and youth
Spreading conspiracy theories just to be famous
I know of one ignoramus, but I'll call him nameless
In fact I think he's somewhat dimwitted or brainless
He's been afflicted by a disease of insaneness
Anyway it's people like this that drive me mad
Making those in the freedom movement look bad
Go away from me please keep your distance
Your a thorn in the side of those in the resistance-
To the global tyranny trying to take us under
Burrying us alive leaving those who slumber to wonder
Is there any lasting value in fighting for freedom?
Phony patriots like you keep us trapped in a global fiefdom!

Freedom Fighter

You rise up in the morning getting set for war
A reality which many people truly abhor
But the truth is evident by the decline of our nation
Suffering from a harsh and rapid deterioration-
Better yet I should say we're being destroyed
Losing many freedoms we once enjoyed
That's why I admonish you fellow soldier
To trust in God with the burden you must shoulder-
In fighting for everything that you hold dear
Yesterday was the moment to conquer your fear-
And launch out into the bloody battlefield
I pray that you as well as I will never yield-
Thus giving way to the trappings of complacency
In an evil system that's the epitome of flagrancy
Don't be hindered by the negative words people say
Accept the challenge Freedom Fighter, be on your way

Fight for Our Dreams

Written upon the heart of every man is a dream
Some simple while others may be extreme
Where would civilization be without the warrior heart?
We'd be missing many treasures and works of art
The global vampires are making it hard for us to exist
Which is why we must band together and resist-
All of the policies that make life a burden
Whether our lives are rural, suburban or urban
Our gifts to the world are unique to our genetic coding
If we keep them inside we begin imploding-
And feeling the pain and weight of lost potential
But when we release them, our growth is exponential
I know life is a struggle just keeping our head above water
We often feel like sheep lead to the slaughter
It's time we strengthen our resolve for our God given vision
Being ready to fight for the fulfillment of our life's mission

Kick Some Tail!

What's it gonna take for Americans to get mad?
And take back our country that's gone sour and bad
Can't we set aside the ballgame for one day?
To learn of how the Globalists want national decay-
Falling all over the land in which we inhabit
America the free has become the land of the Maggot
The price gouging in the US has gone haywire
That's clear as day I'm preaching to the choir
How are we going to put food on the table?
In an economy run by demons whose minds are unstable
Nevermind the idea of enrolling in college-
To help the youth along in pursuing knowledge
Shall single people put away dreams of getting married?
Since every aspect of living is constantly harried
How about we get a backbone and stop moving like snails?
And determine that it's past time to kick some tail!

Still No Word From Osama Yet?

It's been four years now since America was shattered
By a tragedy that left the Big Apple tattered
Yet the global police can't find a clown in a turban
Who's deserving of justice and a mad scourgin'
Doesn't it seem odd that the media has forgotten?
To make mention of a rough reprobate that's rotten
Could it be that's he's dead or just simply missing?
But yet he comes around when our government is pissing-
On our Constitution ready to make moves that are illegal
Regarding us as jackasses that are mindless and feeble
I'm sick of the game that the President is playing-
Along with his cronies who are constanly flambeing-
The truth and trust of the American people
This administration models the meaning of deceitful
Having us believe that Bin Laden was the nemesis
When he's been a CIA asset from his criminal genesis
So then where is America's most wanted man?
Has he run off to form allegiance to the Ku Klux Klan?
Maybe like Elijah he's been miraculously raptured
Or is being tortured in the place where he's captured
If this man is such a treacherous national threat
Shouldn't we wonder why he hasn't been captured yet?

Jeffrey Alexander Hamilton

Shark Bait

How disturbing it was for me to see
That cats and dogs we're used as bait in the sea
Fed to sharks in a cruel show of torture
To the amusement of overindulged porkers-
Fat minded elitist with no respect for life
With mentalities bent and warped like a jackknife
I happen to like dogs, and cats I'll tolerate
I won't stand for God's creatures being treated with hate
Such actions show that our world has hit the skids
Perhaps next they'll come after little kids
If they attempt such action, which I hope the won't
My message to them will simply be "don't"
Because if they do, I'll have to get brutal
To some what I'm saying may sound like flapdoodle
So to those aristocrats here's my simple mandate
Quit using innocent cats and dogs as shark bait

I Will Have a Family Someday

Someday in the future I'll have a big house
Equipped with a garage and good lookin' spouse
We'll enjoy many nights in the dark together
With a bond of matrimony to last forever
Then next will come our four little children
Two boys, two girls, now that's a good fillin'
I'll teach them the ways of Jesus our Lord
How to be kind but ready to wield the sword-
If the New World villains try to steal their liberty
They'll be ready to fight fair and with dignity
My queen and progeny haven't come into fruition
So to the Global Elite I have a simple admonition
Don't you think about crashing my hope of fathering
Even though your plans are dastardly dishonoring
Making it hard for this single man to flourish
And reach my dreams that I plan to nourish-
With prayer mixed in with raw determination
To fight for truth and justice in this dying nation
So before you try to kill me off, let me simply say
I'll keep my faith in God and I will have a family someday

Jeffrey Alexander Hamilton

Goodbye Plastic!

Somehow these days debt seems like the norm
Blasting across our lives like a violent firestorm
Bills as tall as mountains, too numerous to count
With interest rates set at a ridiculous amount
We're under so much pressure to move ahead
But rather than wait we reach for Mr. Plastic instead
So pumped up about the purchase we're going to make
Which seems okay now, but it's a costly mistake
Suppose you lose your job, the card companies don't care
They'll run up your interest leaving you in a financial nightmare
Then to make matters worse, they'll send it to collections
Wanting every amount now, no room for exceptions!
Don't let this demon of debt creep into your domain
Leaving you lifeless and burdened down with pain
But if you have fallen hard, make a firm determination
To join me in getting credit card debt out of our nation

Codex Alimentarius

Here I am eating right trying to live healthy
And live long enough to have a family and grow wealthy
Reaching dreams higher than my own expectations
Then along comes a proposed set of asinine rules and regulations
Treating natural foods as dangerous toxins and chemicals
Big Pharma's trying to overextend it's slimy tentacles
Reaching too far into our daily nutritional decisions
Hoping we'll live life in fear running to our Physicians
Taking out a script for every aching pain and ailment
Sending our food choices to the guillotine of curtailment
Hoping we'll stay dependent on mephitical drugs
While they suck our blood like wild assassin bugs
Meanwhile they'll gladly inject us with mercury and lead
But it doesn't have to be this way, we can be free instead
Free to make decisions as to what vitamins we ingest
Between fluoride and Ginkgo biloba, the latter is easier to digest
Don't make mockery of this message and simply pass it by
For one day you might look back in regret and start to cry
About the time you thought this warning was hilarious
When you live in the prison created by Codex Alimentarius

Microbiologist Murder Mystery

What's behind the death of these microbiologists?
Such a mystery even baffles the minds of criminologists
I'm not one who specializes in the science of biology
But here's a little tidbit from my eagerly anticipated ideology
I'm thinking they knew too much about the Anthrax scare
Or maybe overhead plans for bio-chemical warfare
Could it be that they were about to go public?
Telling America the truth about terror related subjects
I don't know for sure without a book load of facts
But someone has to put this series of tragedies intact
I pray that the Lord will hire a brave investigator
Along with a stalwart and just interrogator
Who will question the President along with his staff
To see if this Anthrax scare was choreographed
Maybe they'll ask about his cabinet taking Cipro
I feel as though such a question could deliver a crushing blow
To the deception that keeps the wool over our eyes
Someone knows what happened, I'm through with the lies
I'm not pointing fingers, I just believe the truth is due
If these scientists were your family, wouldn't you?

FEMA

What happened during that devastating Hurricane?
Did you cut police communication lines for your gain?
No be a good boy and tell America the true story
And go along reveling in your power and vainglory
Then we'll give you a lollipop and pat you on the head
Even though many people lost homes and are now dead
Seriously though, why did you obstruct the water supplies?
And ignore the suffering people with their desperate cries?!
There were elderly, sick people and babies in there
You foul mentally warped criminals, I know you don't care!
You need to be taken before the People and be prosecuted
It's not just that your rescue efforts were poorly executed-
This was a detailed plan to bring in Martial Law
To New Orleans, the city famed for Mardi Gras
I'm through with you thugs and clowns I've little more to say
Just leave America, and let us go about our way!

Neocon Nation

What's all this talk about Republicans or Democrats
When big corporations regard us all like mice and rats
Does it really make a difference who's in the Oval Office?
As long as His actions are deceitful and godless
This new group of men waving the Christian banner
Have taken down America in a cold and cruel manner
They're a group of heartless men bent on world domination
This is no Hollywood movie, it's proven in documentation
The Project for A New American Century makes clear
That these men want to make our freedom disappear
True Conservatives won't destroy our precious land
Given to us by God's gracious yet powerful hand
Millions upon millions have been duped into believing
That these imperialist in the White House are fit for receiving-
Our allegiance in aiding them in their global subjugation-
Of the entire world under the order of the Neocon nation

Repent Church of America

Repent Church of America we're living like wild dogs
Feeding on the poor and helpless like filthy hogs
Stealing from members in our church congregations
Using that money for cars and two week vacations
Pumping our fist glorifying Satanic politicians
Who should truly arouse our deepest suspicions-
With their thirst for blood and hunger for war
They invade one country now they want to take more!
Please Lord Jesus open our very eyes
To the sin we've embraced through deception and lies
Running after every man who mentions God
When for many of these men it's an outright facade
Leading us into a one world religion to kill us
Not before using more terror to chill us
This is not my opinion, but it's a matter of survival
Repent Church of America we're in need of revival

Jeffrey Alexander Hamilton

Land of the Dying Dollar

There was a time when my dollar had worth
Where I could provide for my wife during childbirth
Putting a roof over my family's head was a goal within reach
Even if it wasn't the best looking house in Miami Beach
At least they had basics like shelter, clothing and food-
A good car and a taste of Pappa's tea that was home-brewed
Through hard work I could take them on a nice vacation
A once a year event filled with hugs, kisses and jubilation-
Reuniting with parents, brothers, sisters and cousins
Bringing along their precious children by the dozens
Anyhow I was able to put my kids through school
Some chose the military and I said "I guess that's cool?"
We enjoyed Church on Sundays, learning about the Lord
Choosing to be disciplined buying only what we could afford
I'm an old man now and I see this awful situation
Concerning how the Globalists desire to rob the new generation
Will my children be able to provide for their own?
Or will they sink into the mire of debt trying to keep a home?
I've lived a long life and though I'm no financial scholar
It pains me to see my children living in the land of the dying dollar

Killing Goliath!

Well America, here we stand facing the giant
Will we rebel or give in and be complaint?
Out of fear and intimidation or what we might lose
Today is the day for action while we can still choose-
To stand for what makes our nation bold and strong
Fighting for a right standard while forsaking the wrong
Goliath represents this current evil global system
Pushing his one world agenda of totalitarianism
He mocks the army of God with his tyranny and terror
But he's overstepped his bounds, committing a major error
He stole my country and threatens my prosperity
Making it hard for me and my future posterity
I won't stand for this assault, I'm fighting back
I'm going to be relentless in my counterattack
I've raised my sword and I'm rushing into the war
Join me in killing Goliath, it's his head I'm looking for!

In conclusion, before you're too quick to view these works as nothing but a tie in to a conspiracy theory, I encourage you to check out the information for yourself. Some websites of interest below will help you in your quest for the truth. I may not agree with ALL the information from these websites, but I find them to be highly credible with regard to their presentation of the truth. Each person visiting these sites must and will come to their own conclusions based upon the information presented.

www.thepowerhour.com

www.prisonplanet.com

www.calltodecision.com

www.newswithviews.com

www.propagandamatrix.com

www.fromthewilderness.com

www.freedomabovefortune.com

www.truthtellers.org

www.illuminati-news.com

www.endtheirs.com

www.devvy.com

www.riflewarrior.com

www.mercyseat.net

www.givemeliberty.org

www.infowars.com

www.jackblood.com

www.saf.org

www.militarycorruption.com

www.healthfreedomusa.org

www.vivienkellems.com
www.stopthelie.com

www.sharedhope.org

www.radioliberty.com

www.lighthouseproductionsllc.com

www.mackwhite.com

www.blackgenocide.com

www.savethemales.ca

www.jpfo.org

www.landrights.com

www.861info.com

www.famguardian.org

www.originofaids.com

www.knowledgeofhealth.com

www.nomorefakenews.com

www.americanfreepress.net

www.progressive.org

www.freedom21.com

www.healthline.cc

978-0-595-37050-4
0-595-37050-0

www.ingramcontent.com/pod-product-compliance
Lightning Source LLC
Chambersburg PA
CBHW051410280526
45785CB00003B/1010